MALCOLM SAVILLE'S
SEASIDE
BOOK

By the same author

MALCOLM SAVILLE'S COUNTRY BOOK

MALCOLM SAVILLE'S

Seaside
Book

CASSELL · LONDON

CASSELL & COMPANY LTD
35 Red Lion Square · London WC1

and at

MELBOURNE · SYDNEY · TORONTO · CAPE TOWN
JOHANNESBURG · AUCKLAND

———

Printed and bound in Great Britain
by Jarrold & Sons Ltd, Norwich
F.162

Contents

	Read This First		*page* vii
1.	*The Mighty Sea*		1
2.	*The Magic of the Sea-Shore*		8
3.	*Shells*		19
4.	*Fish*		27
5.	*Sea-Birds*		39
6.	*Guardians of Our Coasts*		52
7.	*Around Our Coasts*		65
8.	*The Road to the Sea*		77
	Index		85

Read This First

IF YOU LOOK at a map of Europe you will see that the British Isles are really very small. And yet they are the most famous islands in all history, and perhaps it is because it is impossible to live anywhere in Britain far from salt water that the sea means so much to us. We have always been a nation of seafarers and sailors.

This is a different sort of book about the seaside and it's been written because I want to help you to have more fun than ever before from a day or a longer holiday somewhere on our magnificent coastline.

You won't find anything here about sailing or swimming because I'm sure both these exciting subjects are better taught to you by your father or mother actually in or on the water. Neither have I anything much to say about big seaside towns, except to remind you that there are always treasures to be found on every beach as the tide slips out twice every twenty-four hours. The birds are different from those of the town and countryside and so are many of the flowers. Every rock-pool is full of life and there are strange seaweeds left on the shingle and the slippery rocks. Then there are hundreds of different shells to be found round our coasts. And when the waves come sweeping up the sand and lap the shingle again, you will wonder, as men have always done, at the marvel of the tides which rise and fall at the call of the moon.

I was born within the sound of the waves of the English Channel only a few miles from where the Norman, William the Conqueror, landed on the Sussex coast and changed our history. Time and time again I have come back to the beaches and cliffs which are home to me, and now I am lucky enough to live only twelve miles from the sea. I have explored, with my own children, much of our coastline, from Northumberland and Yorkshire down the sandy beaches and crumbling cliffs of East Anglia, round the Foreland, past the chalk cliffs of Dover and Eastbourne towards the setting sun and the great granite headlands of Cornwall. I have been lucky enough to see Wales, too, and the glorious western coast of

Scotland. If I had as much time for exploring all over again there would still be new and exciting discoveries to make, and I am sure that there is no thrill like our first glimpse of the sea either from the car, or motor-coach or train at the beginning of a holiday. But really the best way is to hurry on foot down a road which leads to the promenade or a lane which stops at the sand dunes or against a ridge of shingle. And have you noticed that there is no other smell quite as exciting and full of promise as that which blows up the beach and across the sun-drenched street to greet you as you hurry out of the car park or step on to the station platform? Close your eyes now and sniff and perhaps you will be able to remember that magic smell that seems to be a mixture of salt and tar and fish.

The sea is lovely in the summer sun when the air above the beach shimmers in the heat and the little waves sparkle as they topple lazily on to the smooth sand. It is unforgettable at night, too, when the lights of the pier are reflected like drops of coloured fire in the black water, and the moon paints a shimmering path of silver to your feet.

But when the summer dies and the holiday-makers have gone and the deck-chairs are stacked away, the sea changes colour and, with the storms of autumn, becomes a wild and dangerous foe. It batters our coasts, crashes over the deserted promenades and is the enemy of all whose duty takes them on to the water.

There is a common bond between all sailors, but because we live on an island and Britons throughout their history have sailed away to adventure and round the world and back again, we can claim that the sea is the proud heritage of us all. And that means *you* now reading these words, and I hope this book will help you to learn many of its secrets and to enjoy your next seaside holiday more than ever before.

You are sure to find much more than I have room to describe here, and if you would like to write and tell me about your seaside adventures and discoveries, I shall be pleased to hear from you when you get home again. Perhaps we can share some of them and I'll put them in another book one day!

M. S.

Holroyds
Barcombe
near Lewes
Sussex

I

The Mighty Sea

Mysterious, majestic and moody; often tempting, yet with a hidden strength as yet untamed by man, the oceans cover three-quarters of the land surface of our world.

The tides, as they rise and fall, obey the call of our moon. In the black, silent depths of these restless waters strange creatures live and above the waves, hundreds of miles from land, skim lovely little birds like the stormy petrel which you may never see on the shore.

Throughout the world's history mankind has gone down to the sea in ships, and this chapter is to introduce you to some of its wonders and delights and to warn you of its dangers.

HAVE YOU EVER really thought about the power and majesty of the sea? Have you ever realized that nearly three-quarters of the surface of our earth is covered by the oceans and that the mysterious hidden world beneath them consists of mountains and chasms and plains as does the land upon which the human race lives?

As I reminded you at the beginning of this book, the sea, although very pleasant to play by and swim in on a summer's day, can quickly become a dangerous and ruthless foe. From the beginning of time man has had to fight the sea, but he has never tamed it and he never will. He cannot check the rise and fall of the tides nor the power of the winds which can so easily whip the seas to fury. He will, however, surely learn to harness the strength of the tides and use their power to his own purpose before very long. It is possible also that within the lifetime of you, now reading these words, man may be able to explore the bed of the deepest ocean. In January 1960 two brave men—a Frenchman, Dr. Jacques Piccard, and Lieutenant Donald Walsh of the United States Navy —went down to the incredible depth of six and three-quarter miles (35,805 feet) in the Pacific Ocean. The descent was made in a curious vessel called a bathyscaphe specially designed by Piccard's father. Perhaps these two are only pioneers?

The seas close to most of our shores are comparatively shallow. We live on the highest parts of the earth's surface and usually the land beneath the water slopes down gently for some distance. Beyond a depth of 600 feet, however, there is no light, and the cold increases so that it is a marvel that any life exists. But it does. Even below 5,000 feet some curious forms of fish life are to be found, and of course the greater the depth so does the pressure of the water increase.

Although currents, tides and storms disturb the surface of the restless sea, the movement of the water below 200 feet is only very gentle. The mysterious, frightening depths of the dark under-water world are almost placid, because the only movement comes from the deep currents which are caused by the sinking of icy water around the North and South Poles. Slowly these cold currents drift towards the tropical seas round the Equator and the warmer waters they displace rise, and so the movement continues.

Below the surface of our shallow seas are many hidden lands. One such, for instance, is in the middle of our own North Sea and is known as the Dogger Bank. Only about fifty years ago fishermen began to drag their nets (trawling is described later in this book in the chapter on Fish) across the surface of land which was only about sixty feet below the surface. Soon they realized that beneath their keels was a table-land nearly as large as Denmark. They found, too, that this mysterious, hidden land sloped off sharply into much deeper water at the edges, and their trawls brought up bones and peat and fragments of trees, and even some crude stone implements. We are told that the North Sea was once dry land and that Britain was joined to the continent of Europe; and what was found in the trawls of the men who first fished the Dogger Bank proved that on that lost island once lived men of the Stone Age.

Folklore and legend through the centuries suggest that there is a lost land called Atlantis below the waters of the Atlantic Ocean. Tradition says that this was once a great island some distance off the coast of Morocco opposite Mount Atlas. On this island lived a race of men and women of great strength and beauty, and the princes of these people invaded both Africa and Europe, but were finally defeated by the Athenians and their allies. Later, the inhabitants of Atlantis became wicked and impious and the great island was consequently swallowed up in the ocean in a day and a night! Although this story is only a legend, it is exciting and I would like to think that one day it will be possible for man to explore such a lost country under the waters of the Atlantic and perhaps find some traces of a bygone civilization.

Another legendary land now claimed by the sea is the fabled Lemina of the Indian Ocean, and there are others, too, because we know it to be a fact that some of our precious land does, in the course of time, sink below the restless waters.

I wonder if you have ever heard of the mysterious and wonderful Sargasso Sea which is marked on a good atlas between Bermuda and the islands of the West Indies stretching eastwards half-way across the Atlantic Ocean? The Sargasso is certainly one of the wonders of the world, for there is nothing else like it. Throughout recorded history it has been avoided by sailing ships, for it is a vast area nearly as large as the United States, forgotten by the winds of heaven and deserted by those great currents which bring life and movement to the oceans. It is so called because it is virtually a mighty mass of weed called *Sargassum* which has been carried by the currents of the north Atlantic which encircle this strange, silent 'sea'. For millions of years the Sargasso must have existed, floating two or three miles above the floor of the ocean, under the burning sun and cloudless skies of the western Atlantic. Because no flow of fresh water from rivers reaches the weedy wastes of the Sargasso the latter are very salt and a strange animal life, different from all other life known to the naturalists, has established itself there. The weed grows on the rocks along the coasts of the West Indies and Florida and the plants are torn away by hurricanes and drift northward in the Gulf Stream which is the greatest of all the warm-water currents of the oceans. And so, carried, guided and then deserted by the moving waters, millions of tons of *Sargassum* with their many small fishes, crabs and shrimps are brought to a new home. Through the centuries the marine life has changed, adapted and disguised itself to different conditions. Today, if you ventured into the heart of the Sargasso, you would find strange flying-fish which make nests in the weed to contain their eggs looking like the berries of the *Sargassum*. If you searched carefully you would find a snail without a shell, coloured like the vegetation over which it crawls, and there are fierce cannibal fish and great whales too. Some naturalists believe that some of the weeds of the Sargasso have lived for centuries, and although there may be ten million tons of it, it is not really thick enough to trap a vessel. Nevertheless the Sargasso is a strange and mysterious part of the ocean and all sailors agree that it is a place to avoid. I have told you about it because it is one of the many marvels made by the sea.

I have already explained that the surface waters of the seas are never still. They move in currents and in tides. The latter are changeless but the great currents of the oceans may not always have moved in the same direction. The current of most importance to Britain is called the Gulf Stream. This is a moving stream of comparatively warm water which starts its long journey off the West African coast and flows across the Atlantic at a speed of between thirty and sixty miles a day. When it reaches the northeast coast of South America it is travelling nearly a hundred miles a day before flowing into the Gulf of Mexico where it becomes the Gulf Stream. Now look at your atlas if you are interested enough to want to know what happens to this kindly current of warm water. After swirling round the hot Gulf it moves northwards up the North American coast, but when it reaches Greenland, after meeting the cold Labrador current, it fans out south towards the Sargasso, north towards Norway and east to warm our western coasts and those of France and Spain too. And so all the time the waters of the oceans are moving in great streams, some of which are cold and some warm. Their movements are caused by the spinning

4

of our earth, the winds of heaven, the change of temperature and the shape of the continents.

Although the power of the ocean currents is tremendous, it is as little compared to the mysterious forces that control the tides that ebb and flow twice every twenty-four hours. You cannot go anywhere by the sea without being aware of the tides and when we are on holiday at the seaside our days are often planned round them. We know that the tides rise and fall mainly to the pull of the moon and in a lesser degree of the sun, and this is very easy for you to prove for yourself. The moon waxes (grows fat) and wanes (slims down to a thin silvery crescent) each month and as it does so the height of the tide varies. Twice each month, when the moon is at its thinnest, and again when it is full, you will notice that we have the highest of high tides. Such tides are called the springs and you can see the difference in the tides for yourself. You will also realize that the moon rises about fifty minutes later each day than the day before and so the time of high tide is later also. The springs occur when the sun, moon and earth are in a straight line and the combined pull of the heavenly bodies brings the waves far above the normal tide-line on our beaches.

Although I live twelve miles from the coast, we are all very much aware of the springs, particularly if we have had a long, rainy spell and the floods are out. The Sussex Ouse, but a mile from my house which luckily is on higher ground, often overflows its banks. But at the time of the springs when the river is dangerously full the force of the tide at Newhaven is so great that the Ouse cannot run into the sea. Its muddy waters are forced back and the fields and low-lying ground are flooded.

Tides never stop because the earth is always turning and the moon, because it is the nearest big mass of matter to our earth, is always pulling. You may know that all matter is pulled towards other matter everywhere and this force is called 'gravitation'. The moon is matter and so is the sea, and because water can be easily moved the oceans opposite the moon are always pulled up towards it. And while this is happening the earth is spinning too, so that a really great wave of water sweeps over all the oceans, day and night, in answer to this strange call of earth's cold satellite circling for ever round our world.

And so next time you are on the shingle, waiting impatiently for the sand to show, remember the moon! You will understand too what the poet Tennyson meant when he wrote about *moon-led waters*.

A still salt pool, lock'd in with bars of sand;
Left on the shore; that hears all night
The plunging seas draw backward from the land
Their moon-led waters white.

A seaman's life depends upon the direction and strength of the winds of heaven, and it is not possible for any of us to think of the restless sea without remembering the wind. However calm and still the weather may be inland, there is nearly always a breeze on the coast. As long as there has been an earth, masses of air, which we call winds, have swept over its surface and these same winds have always moved the waters of the oceans. It is often a gentle, salty wind that greets us when we hurry down the beach on the first day of the holiday, a happy breeze that sends our little boat skimming over the green waters of the bay; but sometimes it is a terrifying spray-laden force that deafens you and then sucks your breath away and bowls you over, as it crashes the great waves against the promenade in an early autumn gale.

There are winds always moving across the waters just as the familiar currents disturb its restless surface. Winds are affected by the heating up and cooling off of the great land masses of the continents. As you know very well from the forecasts on television and radio, it is now possible to tell fairly accurately what the weather is likely to be. Good seamen always seem to know when a gale is on the way, and for many centuries they have known how to sail their ships with the help of such permanent winds as the North-East Trades in the north Atlantic which blow always between the same latitudes.

Day and night, for as far back in time as we can imagine, the currents, drifts and tides have moved the waters of our earth while the winds of heaven have played on their restless surface. Both wind and sea must always remind us that they have a power which is beyond the wit and skill of man to tame.

I hope I have not bored you by telling you a little of the strength and majesty of the sea. I have tried to show you that you must respect it. As you get to know it better you will learn to love it, but I hope you will never take liberties with it. Although on a hot, calm day it may seem to be your friend as you swim in it or sail on it, the sea is really man's perpetual enemy.

Don't bathe too long in it and remember that girls never seem to get cold as quickly as boys! Come out as soon as you begin to feel and look blue!

Don't go out of your depth without an adult if you can't swim.

Don't bathe too close to a breakwater or groyne in rough weather, and if the tide is high and the waves big, beware of the undertow if the shingle beach shelves down steeply.

Don't go in the sea amongst rocks.

If you're keen on fishing never go out in a boat by yourself. *Never*. A strong tide can carry a small boat out to sea in a few minutes and a broken oar can bring disaster.

Never go out in a boat in foggy weather.

Always take the advice of local people who know the district and what they're talking about. Such people really do know best about tides and currents and where it is safe to bathe.

Don't climb up cliffs in search of birds' eggs and don't go exploring along the shore under the cliffs when the tide is coming in. It's easy to get cut off.

Don't leave bottles, broken glass or tins on the beach.

And finally, in spite of these 'don'ts'—and perhaps because of them—read on now and learn something of the wonders waiting for you wherever the mighty, restless sea breaks against our coasts.

2

The Magic of the Sea-Shore

Just as soon as you run down the steps from the promenade on to the sand or scrunch over the polished, shifting shingle you are in a new world. When you can get away from the crowds on the beach and go off exploring you will find many wonders in every pool, under every rock and even in the sand itself. The sea-shore abounds with a life of its own—strange creatures that walk sideways, little fish in deep pools, shrimps and prawns with curious whiskers, starfish with five arms, jelly-fish which sting and many of those marvels of nature which live in shells. There are curious worms in the sand and animals which look like flowers, and much, much else besides. Read on now and let us look at some together.

As SOON AS the tide begins to ebb it leaves behind it a line of rotting weed and refuse. Amongst this seaweed, on the sand or the smooth stones of the beach you will probably find the SAND-HOPPER which is sometimes, and with good reason, called the beach-flea.

This curious little creature is a distant cousin of the lobster and is khaki-coloured with a hard, crusty back. He has a lot of legs, plenty of whiskers and is a great jumper, and in spite of his appearance he is a valuable member of the sea-shore community. He is useful because he has a big appetite and lives on rotting rubbish and seaweed left by the tide. He is, indeed, a splendid scavenger.

I think that the next sea creature you are likely to find on the beach is the COMMON STARFISH which is recognized easily by its five radiating arms—or are they legs? Seen from above the starfish is pink, but there isn't anything else to see except these curious limbs. He has no face nor mouth on this side of him, but if you turn him over gently—he's quite harmless—you will see how he moves and feeds and lives. On his underside you will notice a broad 'groove' down the centre of each of the five arms. Each of these grooves is filled with little fleshy tubes which are actually the starfish's feet, and with these he creeps along the beach or sea bottom and seizes his prey. You'll be suprised to know that the starfish's favourite meal is oysters, mussels or cockles. It's impossible for a man to open an oyster without a knife, but the starfish does it with his feet. The little tubes are really suckers, and if you could watch him at his meal you would see him raise himself on his five limbs, grip the oyster with them and pull and pull until the two shells are forced apart. The starfish's mouth is actually in the centre of the body disc.

One of the most peculiar things about this strange creature is that, if any of its five limbs are nipped off by a hungry crab, they grow again. So, if you see a starfish with two legs which are shorter than the other three, you'll know that he has had an unfortunate accident, but is recovering!

There's not room in this chapter to tell you about all the other members of the peculiar starfish family except to remind you that there are some more. There's one with a body hardly as big as a penny called the BRITTLE or SNAKE-ARMED STARFISH, with five legs covered with stout spines growing out at right-angles. This strange little creature is most likely to be found under stones or seaweed with his long arms twined round the stones, and I can never understand *why*. When he is touched, the arms tend to break off suddenly.

The SUN STARFISH is the most handsome of them all. He is usually a rich orange-red above and straw-coloured beneath and may have as many as thirteen limbs. His colouring varies, however, and you may find some which are a deep purple with red-tipped, creamy white rays.

In shallow pools where the rocks are shelving and where there is a lot of seaweed, look for the CUSHION STARFISH. He has no long arms or rays but, from above, looks like a plump, curved cushion. He's flat underneath and has tube-like feet like the common starfish.

In a pool with a sandy bottom you may find some tiny but beautiful SAND-STARS each with five delicate, tapering arms covered with scales, but they are difficult to see and rather rare.

The starfish has a near relation called the SEA-URCHIN. The truth is that urchin is another name for hedgehog, and this strange animal, which is sometimes found on the shore, has a body covered with spines which are mounted on joints so that they can be moved in all directions. He has also hundreds of tube-feet like a starfish, and these seem to be arranged in rows of five, like those of his near relation. The sea-urchin has a mouth with very sharp teeth in the centre of the lower surface of its body, and is much appreciated as a delicacy in some parts of Europe, where he is called a sea-chestnut. In colour he is generally purplish pink, and he chews seaweed rather as a rabbit attacks and munches grass.

SEA-CUCUMBERS are another relation of the starfish, but they are not very easy to find between the tide-marks. They are a very peculiar shape, and indeed very often change their shape as they move about in the sea. Sometimes they seem to swell themselves out by filling their bodies with water, and at other times they elongate themselves until they look like slugs or nastily shaped, rough-skinned cucumbers or gherkins. They are not very big— perhaps two to four inches long—and like the little starfish are liable to break into pieces, each of which will grow again into a complete creature. But the sea-cucumber has also a far more remarkable habit, for if it is angry or frightened—or possibly unwell—it has the power to throw off its stomach, intestines and even tentacles! It seems strange that so small and insignificant a form of life should be able to get rid of everything that must make life worth while for it, but the empty skin lies perhaps for months and then begins to grow a body inside it again.

A common and larger form of sea-cucumber is called the COTTON-SPINNER, and when he is fully stretched out he may be a foot long. When alarmed or annoyed he does not discard everything he has, but throws out quantities of cottony-looking matter, which must be part, but not all, of its internal organs. This matter splits up into a mass of white threads which can easily entangle an enemy about to attack it. After using this novel form of defence the cotton-spinner does not seem to be any the worse, and no doubt grows a new set of whatever it is he has discarded.

As the tide goes out it won't be long before you see a member of the crab family. There are several of these to be found on British beaches and they are extremely entertaining to watch. Crabs belong to a family known as *Crustacea*, because the shells on their backs, which are a protective armour, are hard and crust-like. As you know, they scuttle sideways along the sand trying to bury themselves if they sense danger. The commonest is the little green SHORE-CRAB. It has five pairs of legs, the first of which are developed as claws or pincers. The eyes are very peculiar because they are set wide apart between the front pair of claws and stick out like little black buttons.

There's another called the MASKED CRAB which buries himself in the sand as the tide goes out, so you're only really likely to find him when you're digging. He's curiously marked and could give you a sharp nip with his long claws.

But the most interesting of them all is the little HERMIT-CRAB and he has some very odd habits. He is born with armour on the front half of his body but with no protection for the nether portion. Naturally enough, this state of affairs worries the hermit-crab, because although his own nippers are powerful enough, he is afraid that he will be attacked from behind by some creature stronger than himself and cut in half. So he finds himself a home in which he will be safe from his enemies, and his first choice is usually an empty whelk-shell. If, however, the unfortunate whelk is still in occupation and the hermit is desperate, the latter will certainly attack the whelk, tear him to pieces and then take possession. He crawls into the shell backwards, and it is remarkable that his tail seems to be made for this very purpose for it fits well into the spiral curves of the shell!

This crab has another remarkable habit for he sometimes takes a companion, such as a worm, to live with him *inside* his stolen shell. Hermits have also been known to adopt anemones—we shall meet anemones later—and it is amazing that the anemone seems to settle down quite contentedly on the top of a hermit's shell. Although an anemone *looks* like a plant, it is really almost the lowest form of animal life. It has the power to sting and kill other forms of animal life in the sea which the hermit finds edible. So here is a strange partnership, and when the time comes for the hermit to change his home because he has grown too big for the first shell, he actually takes his odd partner and mounts it on to another larger shell.

Between the tides is the time to explore the rocks and the rock-pools and here you will find many strange creatures besides the members of the starfish family mentioned earlier. As you climb across the slimy timbers of an old breakwater or over the rocks, take care not to cut your feet on the barnacles which, difficult though it is to believe, are actually animals belonging to the same family as crabs and lobsters. There are two kinds of barnacles, and the sort you are likely to see on the rocks are called ACORN-BARNACLES. You will notice the little tent-like shells, made up of six 'armoured' plates with a hole at the top. The barnacle starts his strange life as a tiny swimming creature, rather like a minute lobster, and during the end of April you will find the water in the rock-pools alive with them. Some of these strange infants eventually attach themselves by their heads to the rocks and proceed to grow their armour. They keep their legs free and use them to kick food into their mouths. Once the barnacle has fixed himself to the rock or the breakwater nothing will shift him.

There is another type of barnacle called the GOOSE-BARNACLE or STALKED BARNACLE, and this is found on floating logs or on ships under the water-line. It is a strange-looking animal, for it has a fleshy stalk with a flattish body protected by five plates. This is the barnacle which can slow down the pace of a great ship and send it into dry dock to be cleaned before the next voyage. Once there were many strange legends told of this barnacle, and for a long time it was believed that young geese were hatched out of these odd-looking shells.

Perhaps the most remarkable form of life to be found in a pool are the SEA-ANEMONES. They have been sometimes called 'living flowers of the sea', and there are many different sorts to be found round our shores. Probably the most common is the BEADLET which lives almost anywhere between the tide-marks but prefers a pool. It is reddish brown, sometimes with blue spots, with a wide base fixed firmly to the rock, then an upright column and a disc from which the tentacles wave and hide the mouth in the centre.

Anemones are almost always beautiful and highly coloured and it is true that they *look* like flowers. They fix themselves to a rock or shell or even to a piece of vegetation and then set about satisfying a greedy appetite.

The tentacles of the anemone surround the creature's mouth, and are armed with minute poison glands. Whenever a tiny fish or even a small crab touches one of the waving tentacles, all the others lean towards the victim, which is seized, stung with poison and instantly conveyed to the anemone's mouth, which is a slit at the top of the column or 'stalk'. Although the anemones round our coasts are small, you will, if you touch one with your little finger, feel the slight pull of the tentacles.

A naturalist once gave a small anemone a halfpenny. Instead of rejecting it, however, as he had expected, the strange creature spread its mouth round the coin and worked its body round it, with the result that it was cut in two. But not even being cut in two could kill the anemone, for the two halves grew into two perfect new anemones. They do not usually reproduce themselves in this way, although sometimes new anemones 'bud off' from the foot stalk. It seems as if, usually, eggs are laid and hatched in the parent's body, and the babies swim out when ready. Some anemones live quite well in captivity, provided they are given enough to eat. Anemones live for a very long time, and some have actually been kept alive in an aquarium for sixty years.

SHRIMPS and particularly PRAWNS are sometimes found in rock-pools, but the best way to catch both is with a shrimping-net when the tide is at its lowest. Push the net along before you in knee-deep water and you will be amazed at what you will pick up. These shallow waters are the nurseries of many baby fish and crabs, but your haul will almost certainly be mainly shrimps and prawns and when you examine them you will see that they are very peculiar-looking creatures.

Shrimps and prawns belong to the same *Crustacea* family as crabs and lobsters. There are many different kinds of shrimps, but many of those sold in the fish shops are not shrimps at all but baby prawns, which when boiled turn bright pink. Shrimps when boiled turn a dark speckled brown, and are just as tasty to eat, but they are always smaller than prawns and rarely longer than two and a half inches.

Shrimps are more likely to be found closer in to the shore, but they are almost invisible in the water, for they seem to change colour to match the sand over which they are swimming, and sometimes they are nearly transparent. If you stand very still and the water is calm and clear, you may see them swimming at a great pace round your bare toes, and will notice that they seem almost to leap through the water by pushing with their powerful tails. Sometimes the shrimp buries itself quite deeply in the sand; it has a tremendous appetite for its size, and will feed off almost any garbage thrown into the sea or found on the sea-shore.

Prawns like deeper water but you are almost certain to bring up some in your net, and you will see the difference between them and shrimps at once. Not only is the prawn bigger—full-grown he may be five to six inches in length—but his longer, more slender feelers are actually of a greater length than his body. He is wonderfully graceful and agile, and some naturalists have called him 'the fairy of the rock-pools'. His usual colour is a greyish white with touches of brighter colour such as brown and red.

Another discovery you might make in a rock-pool between the tide-marks is a LOBSTER which is another crustacean. Although this curious and most ridiculous-looking creature is bright and scarlet when you see him on the fishmonger's slab, in life his colour is greenish blue. Some fishermen say that the lobster's colour matches his surroundings and they can tell from which part of the coast he comes. Unlike the crab, the lobster has a very powerful tail which he uses to propel himself, either backwards or forwards, through the water.

The lobster is a very good mother. Her eggs—or berries as they are sometimes called—are attached to her broad tail, and are carried round with her in this position even for a time after they have hatched. While the infant lobsters are growing up their mother looks after them rather as a hen does her chicks. At the slightest sign of danger she rattles her big claws, and her babies scuttle under her body for safety. She has an odd habit of being able to throw off or discard her claws when she is badly frightened. There does not seem any object in doing this, but you will remember that the starfish can grow another ray, and sometimes the crab casts several legs and grows them again. The lobster does the same with her claws.

So much for the rock-pools. You will probably find many more fascinating forms of life in a pool than I have been able to describe if you sit down by it and quietly watch the water. Watch the crevices too, and if you move any small rocks under which a sea creature may be sheltering be sure to replace them.

I must warn you of two dangers on the shore. The first is an unpleasant little fish called the WEEVER or VIPER-FISH which buries itself in the sand. It has poison in the spines which run along its back, just as a snake secretes it in his fangs. A sting from the weever can be very unpleasant, and should you be unlucky enough to be stung, treat it as you would a bee-sting—put on ammonia or a blue-bag.

The other danger is the JELLY-FISH which I have heard called a 'submarine ghost'. The blob of shapeless jelly which you some-times find on the shore as the tide runs out is a dead jelly-fish. Actually it is not a fish but an animal like the anemone with the same power to sting. To see a jelly-fish in all its beauty you should watch the water at high tide from the end of the pier or from a harbour wall. Only then will you see their lovely colours and strange and beautiful shapes, as they drift a few feet below the surface, opening and shutting a bell-like disc which looks rather like a mushroom or umbrella.

A jelly-fish has no bones, and looks as though it is little more than a mass of tissue enclosing a considerable quantity of water. Between the upper and lower sides of the 'umbrella' are a number of fairy-like arms or tentacles, each of which carries a sting.

The commonest jelly-fish in British waters is a lovely violet-blue. Although it is not much bigger than a soup-plate, it can sting you unpleasantly, so it is always wise to avoid them when bathing.

Another type is the amber-coloured jelly-fish which sometimes come into the shallow water at the mouths of rivers and may break the salmon nets with their weight. Some of these are quite big, with tentacles that stream out behind them in the water for several yards.

As soon as the jelly-fish is exposed to air and sun the water in its strange body evaporates, until even the shapeless blob which we saw first on the beach has disappeared.

Now I must tell you something about the SEAWEEDS of which you will find many strands and bunches left by the tide on the shore, or which are 'anchored' to the rocks or wooden piles of the breakwaters. Seaweeds do not grow in the same way as do plants on land which have roots and draw some of their nourishment from the soil.

Seaweeds get their food from sea water, and, although some-times they appear to be rooted, they only fix themselves to something solid so that they can withstand the force of the tide and waves.

Seaweeds need sunlight and flourish best near the shore. As life began in the sea, seaweeds were undoubtedly the first known plants on our planet and there are three main types of them. They are easy to recognize as they are in three colour groups—green, brown and red. The green grow close to the shore and are covered only at high tide. The brown varieties grow mostly between the tide-marks, while the red seaweeds flourish in much deeper waters, although oddly enough you may find some red specimens flourishing amongst the brown, which seem to protect them. Each type of seaweed is the colour best suited to the depth of water in which it lives.

Some kinds of seaweeds are edible, and the large brown types give us iodine which has a food-value besides being antiseptic. Until a comparatively short while ago all the iodine in the world came from seaweed which was dried in the sun and then burnt in big pits built in the sand and lined with stones. Iodine is an important chemical, and we cannot do without it, for it helps to build up a gland in our bodies which largely controls our growth and intelligence. Animals seem to know by instinct that seaweed is good for them, for sometimes in certain parts of the country sheep and cows come down to the beach at low tide and scramble amongst the rocks to eat the weed.

With a little trouble you can take home a splendid memento of your seaside holiday in the form of a seaweed collection, but you will have to take some trouble if it is to be a success.

The seaweeds which you will notice first on the beach will probably be parts of the coarser, bigger, brown types which have been torn from their moorings by the waves and left stranded on the high-tide mark. Amongst this flotsam you will be certain to find the commonest of our seaweeds, which is called BLADDER-WRACK and is easily recognized by its fronds and 'air-blisters'. If you could see the complete plant you would be amazed at its size, for it has been known to reach a height of ten to eleven feet. It dries black.

The green seaweeds are mostly thread-like or net-like, although some remind us of ferns. The red group, which are often on the low-tide level, are the loveliest of them all—very light and delicate and often nearly transparent. Some are like moss and some almost like coral, and these are the types which will make your collection really worth while.

You will not want much equipment besides a stick with a crooked handle for pulling in pieces of floating weed, a sharp knife

The Sea-Urchin is a near relative of the starfish. Urchin is another name for hedgehog, and this strange animal has a body covered with spines that can move in all directions

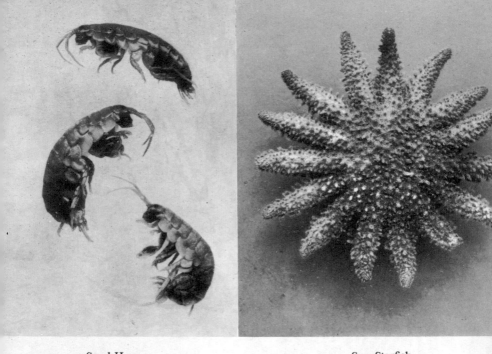

Sand-Hoppers

Sun Starfish

Common Starfish

Brittle Starfish

Sea-Cucumber

Goose-Barnacles are often found on floating logs or on ships under the water-line. They are strange-looking animals, for they have fleshy stalks with flattish bodies protected by five plates

and a bag in which to carry your specimens. Rinse off as much sand and dirt as you can in rock-pools or in the sea before taking your specimens home where you should have a really large basin or bath full of sea water. Some seaweeds decompose quickly if put into fresh water, so your specimens should be thrown at once into the bath and washed thoroughly again. You will also need another smaller basin—white if possible—also filled with sea water, together with some sheets of white cartridge-paper cut to sizes suitable for mounting your specimens. If you can buy a sheet of perforated zinc—the sort that is used for making the sides and door of a meat-safe would do splendidly—this will be a help.

Now put a few of the seaweeds into the smaller basin, place a sheet of cartridge-paper on to the zinc, and slip them both into the basin and under the specimen you wish to mount. When the paper is directly under the piece of seaweed, raise your 'tray' an inch or so, taking care not to disturb the fronds too much, and while it is still under water arrange the specimen to your liking with a clean paint-brush. You can also use a pair of sharp scissors under water to trim off any ugly pieces of stalk. When you have arranged it as nicely as possible, raise the tray gently right out of the water, trying not to disarrange the specimen.

If you can persuade your mother to let you have some butter-muslin, spread some ready on sheets of blotting-paper. Slide your wet cartridge-paper off the zinc tray on to the muslin. Now do your best to mop up the water still remaining on the paper, then cover it with another piece of muslin and more blotting-paper. Your specimen is now ready for pressing, and perhaps the best way of doing this is under a pile of heavy books. After a few hours the blotting-paper sheets above and below the seaweed must be changed, but the muslin should not be moved. You must keep up the pressure for about four days and after this change the blotting-paper perhaps once a day. When at last the muslin is removed, the seaweed itself, which should now be quite dry, can be transferred to a new sheet of dry paper and mounted by means of a little gum or even with tiny strips of transparent paper.

Thicker, coarser seaweeds like the bladder-wrack could not be treated this way. It would probably be better to wash these under the tap, remove the salt, and then dry between old towels before pressing in the way described above.

Try to keep all the same kinds—green, red or brown—together, and, even if you don't know the names of them all, write down the date and place in which they were found.

You will be surprised, at the end of a fortnight by the sea, to see how many different specimens you have collected.

I hope I have told you enough about what you may find on the sea-shore to start you off exploring. Remember that every tide brings us something different and every rock-pool swarms with unfamiliar life.

3

Shells

One of the most unforgettable pictures in the world is by an Italian painter called Botticelli and shows Venus, the Goddess of Beauty, rising in a delicate scallop-shell from the sea. I have seen this picture in Florence in Italy and I hope that you, too, will have this experience one day.

Sea-shells, with their perfection of form, design and colour have inspired artists through the ages. And always people everywhere have collected them for their beauty and use.

They are the treasures of the deep, but wherever you go at the edge of the sea you will find some at your feet. You can collect shells yourself as a souvenir of your holiday, so I tell you now a little about a few of the most common to be found around our shores.

As the tide slips down the beach it leaves for you a collection of sea-shells of all sizes, shapes and colours. If you dig in the sand with your fingers you will find still more shells and fragments of shells, and millions more are being pulled up from the ocean bed every day and strewn, like a sort of magic offering, along our beaches for you to find.

Shells are the little houses made by the creatures which live in them. These creatures are *not* fish because no fish makes a shell and no inhabitant of a shell has a backbone, or indeed any bones at all. The Latin name for the creatures that live in shells is *Mollusca* and there are some, like the snail, which live on the land.

We are sure that molluscs are a very low form of life which lived in the sea long before the first fish appeared. We know this because shells have often been found on mountainsides proving they were left there when the sea covered most of the earth.

Shells are made of lime which is brought into the sea by rivers and streams. Centuries of running water have teased at the lime-stone rocks and washed the deposits of lime down into the sea bed, and here—we do not know how many tens of thousands of years ago—the first mollusc began to absorb lime into his system. Every one of these soft creatures—they are really like slugs—is covered with a loose fold of flesh rather like a cloak. This cloak is called the mantle and has very remarkable properties. It *makes* the shell by taking from the blood of the mollusc the lime which was first absorbed from the water, and converting it into shell. This it does by mixing the tiny particles of lime with a kind of glue which hardens into the armour of a shell. It is wonderful to realize that as the soft sea-slug grows, so does his mantle grow with him, and as it grows it goes on making shell, so that the mollusc is always protected and always has a shell to fit him. The layer of shell next to the mollusc's body is always smooth and 'satiny' and often glows with lovely colours. This layer is called 'mother-of-pearl'.

When a mollusc dies, the soft and defenceless body inside the shell dissolves slowly away. Soon the shell, now very much lighter and no longer fixed to a rock or to seaweed, is pulled along by the tide and eventually thrown up on some beach.

You will soon see that shells are of two main types—a shell all in one piece like that of a snail or a whelk or a limpet, and shells in two pieces, such as the common mussel, razor-shell, or oyster. The first are known as univalves—easy to remember since *uni* means 'one'—and the second bivalves, which always have two saucer-like shells. Think of them as the two wheels of a bicycle, and you will remember which sort are the bivalves!

The univalves move about the sea and shore more than the bivalves, and they progress in a very odd way by means of what is called a 'foot'. Sometimes this foot is strong enough for the mollusc to pull itself along, and sometimes it is so shaped that it acts rather like a pair of oars. The bivalve's foot is more like a thick tongue, and is used for burrowing into the sand or actually jumping along it. Some of these creatures, however, rarely move, and these have no visible foot.

The ridges on shells and their texture are due to the speed at which the mantle converts the lime into shell, and any irregularity in the surface which you handle corresponds with an irregularity in the mantle. Some molluscs make their shells more quickly than others, and you may be interested to know that the two shells of a bivalve mollusc known as the giant clam sometimes weigh more than five hundred pounds. I used to wonder what puts the *colour* into a shell, for lime is white and always has been, but the answer is that the mantle of every mollusc contains certain dyes which colour the lime which it is making into shell. Surely the making of a shell is one of the greatest marvels of nature! It seems almost impossible that the boneless blob of jelly which is the mollusc should be able to make those exquisite shapes in delicate colour-ings which we can pick up for ourselves on any beach. Let me tell you now of some of those which you will be most likely to find.

The RAZOR-SHELL is perhaps the easiest of all shells to recognize. It is long, straight, and handsomely coloured in yellowish green. Sometimes you may find one as long as eight inches, but the average length is six inches. You will see at once that the razor is a bivalve. It is also a burrower, and its shape enables it to force itself down into the sand easily. If you can find a 'live' razor-shell on the beach—look for one half out of its burrow—watch to see how quickly it can disappear. As soon as it is placed on the sand, you will see that its white foot will be stuck out to its full length beyond the shell and that its pointed tip will begin to burrow into the sand, soon taking the shell after it. You will see now that the narrow shape of the shell offers little or no resistance, and the 'razor' can disappear almost before you can turn round.

There are several different sorts of razor-shells, and you will find that the colours vary, too. If you can find a perfect specimen, it is very attractive.

The PIDDOCK, a strange mollusc, with a whitish shell about

six inches long. It has the astonishing habit of being able to burrow into stone and timber. You may find some piddocks sticking out of a rock or the wood of a breakwater and notice that the two shells do not seem big enough to hide completely the white body of the mollusc within. From one end of the shell you will see the creature's siphons protruding, and you must realize that all molluscs of this type live by taking in water by one of these siphon-like tubes and expelling it through the other, after the oxygen on which they live has been extracted.

The piddock makes his burrow by twisting and rocking his shell against the rock. If you look carefully you will notice that the edges of his shell are a mass of short, sharp points rather like the edge of a saw. As he bores he blows out the powdered rock through the exhaling siphon tube and holds on inside the burrow with his foot. The only purpose of all this hard work seems to be a desire to hide, for just as soon as the burrow is as big as himself, he stops work!

You are most likely to find the piddock when holiday-making on the South Coast. Look for him near the low-tide mark where there are chalk cliffs or where the rock of the pools is soft, for although he is strong he does not like to work harder than he need, and so avoids the harder rocks of the north.

The piddock has another unusual habit, for he gives off a strong bluish white light at nights. Many fish and sea-animals do this, of course—this light is called phosphorescence—and hundreds of these tiny piddocks in a rock-pool remind us of the pin-points of stars against the velvet sky of a summer night.

The MUSSEL is very common, and there is a fresh-water variety as well. The shell is about three inches long—smooth and oval and bluish in colour. It is a bivalve, and if you can find one at rest you will see that the two halves of the shell gape a little, showing the soft body of the mussel within. When the mussel is alarmed, however, the shell closes almost with a snap, and sends out a squirt of water. It moves slowly by means of a slender foot which appears from the straighter side of the shell, and it can anchor itself to surrounding stones or rocks by a 'rope' of tiny threads which appear to issue from the mysterious foot. There are some mussels which are nice to eat, and fishermen use them as bait for bigger fish, too. The edible mussel seems to like the mouths of rivers, probably because it lives on some of the refuse brought down to the sea; perhaps one day you will see one of the great mussel beds. Countless thousands of mussels fasten themselves to the smooth rocks and there deposit a residue of fine mud. As the mud bank grows, the mussels lengthen the threads by which they are anchored, and so rise above the stifling mud.

You are not very likely to find OYSTER shells on an ordinary beach, but on some river estuaries, particularly those of Essex, the oyster is farmed commercially, as it is such a delicacy. I am sure you are familiar with the brownish, flat, irregular shell, and know that sometimes pearls are found inside an oyster shell. The oyster is a near relation to the mussel, and its shell is very strong indeed and impossible to force apart without a knife. The lining to the oyster's shell is lovely mother-of-pearl, but real pearls are not found in the oysters bred in British waters.

The GREAT SCALLOP is a splendid shell to find and is probably the largest you will see on any British beach, because its average size is six inches long by five inches wide. The two shells are not the same size, for the lower is curved while the upper is flat. Both are very prettily coloured—the lower usually being pink and yellow, while the flatter shell is more highly coloured in browns and reds. Both shells are solid and strongly ribbed, and rather remind us by their shape of an open fan. In many seaside places you will see scallop shells used as borders to garden flower-beds or as drinking-baths for birds.

There are many types of British scallops smaller than this one, and you will find them all very attractive both in shape and colour, and I think you will recognize them easily. The scallop is one of the few molluscs with the power of moving fast through the water, and he manages this by rapidly opening and closing his shells like a giant mouth.

The LIMPET is probably the easiest to find of the univalve single shells; each is inhabited by a mollusc with a strong foot by which it propels itself along in its search for food. The limpet shell is conical, but not spiral like that of a snail, and although you will sometimes find limpets washed up on the beach, you are more likely to see them fixed firmly, with thousands of others, to rocks which are covered with water at high tide. Until you have tried to pick a limpet off the rocks with your fingers you will not realize how firmly he can anchor himself with his strong foot, which acts as a sucker. If the limpet does not hear you coming and does not feel in danger, you *may* be able to dislodge him by a sudden, side-ways wrench.

Although the limpet leaves his unusual home when the tide comes in, it is strange that he should always go back to *exactly* the same spot on the rock to anchor himself again. He never makes a mistake and goes to the wrong niche, for the shallow little hole to which he clings exactly fits the edges of his shell.

Some of the loveliest little shells which you will find on our beaches are aptly named after the beautiful goddess, Venus, and are deep burrowers in mud and sand. It is strange that the shells of such creatures, which are rarely seen alive on the surface of the beach, should be so beautifully coloured, but we must be grateful when we find some of them on the low-tide mark. In tropical waters the VENUS shells are often very large, but you are not likely to find any more than an inch and a half across. The shell is round and triangular-shaped, and although the tints vary a great deal— yellow, red, pink and even brown—you will see that the bands of colour run round the shells in circles. Some types of venus shells are marked with crosswise zigzags of purple or chestnut or reddish 'rays'. As I said, you will hardly ever find a live venus, but many of the shells are washed up by every tide, particularly on our south and west coasts.

Another burrowing mollusc which is easy to recognize is the COCKLE, with its two even, rounded shells. These shells are very beautifully curved and almost heart-shaped. This was recognized long ago, for the cockles belong to the family with the Latin name *Cardium*, which comes from the Latin for 'heart'.

Cockles are good to eat and are also much used by fishermen for bait. They live buried in the sandy mud, generally a few feet beyond the low-tide mark, but they have another, rather amusing, habit. You will remember that I have already told you how these creatures use their one foot for burrowing into the sand or for moving along it. The cockle has a particularly powerful foot, and sometimes you may see a number of them bounding over the wet sands towards the incoming tide like tiny kangaroos. The cockle must be the liveliest of all our molluscs and the commonest member of the family is the prickly cockle. The size of the shell is about one and a half inches; it is strongly ribbed and each square-topped rib bristles with spines. The background of the shell is yellowish-white with bands of rusty red.

There are two kinds of PERIWINKLE, the rough and the common. They have *spiral* shells, and both are very attractive because the colours vary so much. The shells of the rough peri-winkle are only about half an inch high, and you will find them usually on rocky coasts which are covered with bladder-wrack seaweeds. This seaweed is the rough periwinkle's favourite meal,

The most remarkable form of life to be found in a pool is the Sea-Anemone. Here are sea-anemones with some Limpets which anchor themselves firmly to rocks which are covered at high tide

Shore-Crab

Masked Crab

The Jelly-Fish is not a fish but an
animal like the anemone with the
same power to sting

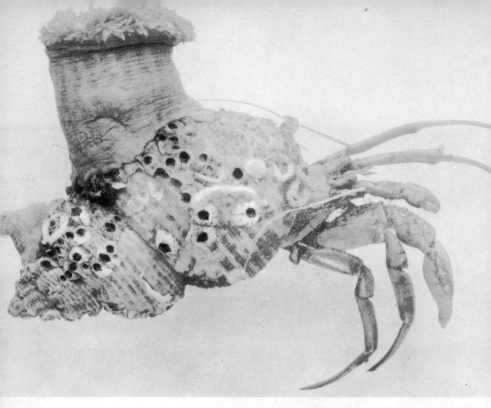

Hermit-Crab in a whelk-shell with passenger anemone

Acorn-Barnacles

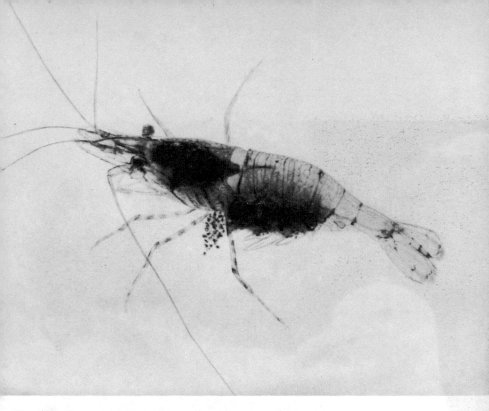

Prawn

Shrimp

The Herring-Gull is the commonest of the gulls, and can be found
nearly everywhere at the seaside and sometimes inland, too, on water
and the farmer's fields

Lobster

Bladder-Wrack

The smallest of the gulls is the Black-Headed Gull, foolishly named, because in winter the head is white!

and if you search carefully in such places you may pick up his shells in white, yellow, orange, red, purple or even black.

The common periwinkle is a bigger brother. The spiral of his shell is sharper and his colours are not quite so gay. Sometimes he is brown or red, but more often black.

The COMMON WHELK is another mollusc much valued as a food and as bait. This shell is the commonest of the larger, spiral shells you will find on the beach. The average length is perhaps two inches, but in deep water you might find specimens of six inches. It is common everywhere, but very abundant in the north, where Scottish children call them buckies. The shells are nearly always beautifully coloured and of a brownish tint.

Another member of this family is the DOG-WHELK, which is also very common around our coasts. At low tide look for them clinging to dry rocks, and then quite suddenly letting go and falling with a 'plop' into the pool beneath.

The whelks are flesh-eaters, and their favourite meal is another mollusc, which they attack in rather a disgusting way. Having found a succulent-looking oyster for his dinner, the whelk drills a neat, round hole in his victim's shell. This he does with his tongue, which is like a long, flexible file—a tongue so long that the whelk does not use it all at the same time, but keeps some in reserve, until his teeth at the far end of the saw are worn out! When the hole is deep and wide enough, the whelk withdraws the saw and inserts instead a long, flexible snout, through which he sucks the soft and defenceless body of the oyster.

Dog-whelks are also natural scavengers, and help to keep the sand between the tide-marks clear of dead sea creatures.

Your Shell Collection

I hope I have told you enough to interest you in making a collection of sea-shells for yourself. Be sure to keep only clean, unbroken shells, and always be on the look-out for a better, bigger specimen than the one you have. If you are lucky enough to find a shell with its occupant still living, you will have a better specimen than one which has been thrown up by the tide. You must remove the mollusc carefully and then soak the shell in hot water to remove the salt and dirt. When dry it is a good idea to paint your shells over with gum arabic or varnish, so that they gleam as they did in the water.

If you can collect enough match-boxes you may be able to make a miniature cabinet in which to house your collection. The shells will look well resting on their beds of white cotton-wool, and you should label each box with the name of the specimen and the place and date of finding. Of course you will need larger boxes for the larger specimens.

Perhaps one evening in winter, or during a holiday week-end when it is too wet to go out, your collection of shells will help to bring back memories of lovely golden days or peaceful evenings as you followed the tide out and found some of the treasures thrown up to mortals by Father Neptune himself.

4

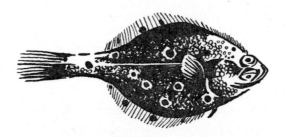

Fish

What joy attends the fisher's life!
  Blow, winds, blow!
The fisher and his faithful wife!
  Row, boys, row!
He drives no plough on stubborn land,
His fields are ready to his hand;
No nipping frosts his orchards fear,
He has his autumn all the year!

The husbandman has rent to pay,
  Blow, winds, blow!
And seed to purchase every day,
  Row, boys, row!
But he who farms the rolling deeps,
Though never sowing, always reaps;
The ocean's fields are fair and free,
There are no rent days on the sea!

I found these verses in an old book of sea-songs. Because they do give a good idea of the freedom of the sea, of those who live and work on it and of the fun and excitement of fishing, I thought you would like to read them.

FISH ARE ABOUT the oldest back-boned creatures in our world. We know that they are amongst the earliest forms of life and yet they cannot, as you know, live on land. Everything living must have air or die and yet, just as we die of suffocation if we are held under water, so is a fish suffocated *in* the air. A fish has no lungs by which it can breathe air. Instead it has gills with which it is able to extract the air that is contained in water.

Fish are cold-blooded. Some are able to distinguish colours but do not seem to be able to hear very well. We know that they *feel* vibrations in the water. Newly born young of animals (and humans) are always fed by the mother but baby fish have to find their own food or die. A few fish give birth to living young ones, but most lay eggs in the water.

From earliest times man has fished so that he might live and today in Britain more people—men, women and children—fish for fun than take part in any other kind of sport. All round our long and exciting coastline in all kinds of weather at all times of the year you will see people fishing. *You can do the same* and I hope this chapter will start you off on the wonderful sport of sea-angling. There's not much you can do at the seaside when it is really wet except get into oilskins and fish off the pier or even from the beach. You can even fish at night, and really keen anglers never seem to mind getting wet and cold.

Nobody knows how many untold millions and millions of fish there are in our seas. Some are large, some small, some beautiful and graceful and some as ugly as sin itself. There are some fish which give an electric shock while others have poisoned fins. Some are only to be found in deep water while others come close to the land. In our waters I suppose there are at least fifty different kinds of sea-fish, and I'm going to tell you about some so that you'll recognize them when you see them.

Fishing for a living is still done from most of our coastal towns and villages, and if you watch the fishing boats unloading their slippery, glistening cargoes on to the quay it's more fun if you know what the crews have brought in. It's from the east coast that most of our big fishing fleets go out and it's a wonderful sight to see them coming home. I remember watching a fleet come racing to the safety of Whitby harbour in a gale and I've seen them come into Lowestoft too. Smaller vessels fish the waters of the English Channel, and off Devon and Cornwall there are some fleets fishing specially for pilchards. Sometimes you can watch a few small boats hauled up a sloping beach by a wire cable, and there is always a thrill in seeing the fish come in and an even greater thrill in fishing yourself. But before I give you some hints on sea-angling you may like to know how the professional fishermen sets about his job. It's a very tough job indeed, and it's not surprising that there are no weaklings amongst the men who brave storms and the icy Arctic waters to bring you your fish for dinner. It's as well to remember that just as there are families of plants, birds and animals so there are three different fish families—demersal, pelagic and the shellfish.

First, the *demersal* fish which live on or near the bed of the sea. The best known of these are the 'flatties' such as sole, plaice, turbot, flounders and dabs. Round fish such as haddock, whiting and the valuable cod also belong to this family.

Fish that swim near the surface of the sea are called *pelagic* and include herring, mackerel, pilchards, sprats and the tiny whitebait.

Finally, there are the shellfish of which there are two kinds—*molluscs* such as oysters, mussels, scallops and other hard-shelled sea creatures, and *crustaceans*, including those with horny outer coverings like shrimps, prawns, lobsters and crabs.

Different sorts of fish are caught in different parts of the sea by different methods. More than half of the total catch of white fish landed at British ports each year is caught by deep-sea trawlers from Hull and Grimsby on the east coast and from Fleetwood in Lancashire. A trawler is so called because it hauls a trawl net along the bed of the sea. These big deep-sea boats with all their gear and modern gadgets cost at least £200,000 each and up to £300 a day for maintenance when at sea. The average voyage is twenty-one days. It takes five and a half days to reach the fishing grounds off Iceland, Greenland, northern Norway, Bear Island and the Barents Sea and the same time to get home again after leaving ten days for fishing. Once the fish are found and fishing begins, every member of the crew is working most of the day and night, although there is a wise regulation that each man must rest for six hours after an eighteen-hour spell on deck. All the fish caught are gutted and cleaned at once and then packed in ice and the livers are collected and processed for oil—your cod-liver oil to keep colds away! Imagine working with numbed hands gutting icy fish on a heaving deck through the bitter, long Arctic night, in danger from stormy seas and drifting ice floes. No wonder they call this a man's job.

Near-water trawlers vary in size from seventy to 140 feet and many are now powered by modern diesel engines. They fish chiefly in the North Sea, the English Channel and the Irish Sea. The larger vessels in this group stay at sea for ten to fourteen days. Some of the smaller boats are motor-powered cobles with a crew of three. These fish at night only a few miles from the shore.

The inshore fishermen work round our coasts in small boats usually owned by a family or a small syndicate. Such boats are those that we see fishing off the south coast and the sort you are most likely to notice when on holiday. Many fine fish such as sole and plaice are caught from boats like these with nets and long baited lines. Our inshore fishermen catch nearly all our supplies of crabs, lobsters and other shellfish.

Before I tell you how fish are actually caught, I must mention particularly the drifters used specially for the herring harvest. They are called 'drifters' because they use the drift-nets described below. They fish mostly off the east coasts of Scotland and England. These sturdy vessels are between seventy-five and ninety feet in length. The smaller ones are usually made of wood and are owned and manned by a family, while the larger are of steel and owned by a company. Each craft has radio so that the skipper is in touch with the shore and the rest of the fleet, and an echo-sounder to record shoals of herring directly below the drifter.

There are several ways in which the fisherman catches his fish. *Lining* is the name given to the method of using a long line of baited hooks, one end of which is fixed to a floating buoy or marker and the other to the boat itself.

Drifting is used for pelagic fish (as the herring) with nets that drift with wind and tide. These nets are marked with buoys and are kept upright with cork floats. When the nets have been 'shot' from the drifter, one and a half miles of buoys may stretch in the wake of the vessel which drifts in the darkness until hauling begins.

Seining is becoming much more popular and is a very ingenious method. First the vessel pays out warp to which the net is attached on a triangular course from and back to a marker buoy. As the boat then moves forward, the net is hauled in.

Finally, the most successful method of all is *trawling*. The trawl itself is like a big net bag held open at the mouth by 'otter boards' and by the pressure of wind and tide. This trawl-net is towed about two hundred yards behind the trawler, and the fish enter it by the open mouth and are trapped in what is called the 'cod-end'. About every two hours the heavy trawl is hauled in on a winch. When the net is aboard, the mouth of the cod-end is drawn tight so that it can be swung over the pounds into which the catch is dropped.

Now do you feel like fishing yourself? If your father or elder brother is keen and experienced, you won't want to hear anything more from me. You'll just watch them and they'll be glad to teach you. Various sorts of fish are caught off different parts of our coast, and the people to tell you where and when to fish, and what you are most likely to catch are the boatmen on the beach or the man in the shop that sells fishing tackle. From people who live in the place and have been fishing for years you will learn far more than I can tell you in a book.

But in case you would like to know enough to want to know more, here are a few tips.

Sea-angling is particular fun because if you're not afraid of rough weather you can fish all the year round. You can fish from a pier, from a breakwater, from the beach or from a boat in deeper water. I cannot advise you about the sort of tackle to use because I don't know where you are going to start. Again you must ask an experienced grown-up for advice. And what you use also depends on how much money you have to spend, but you will certainly want at least one rod and possibly two. You'll want a stronger rod and line if you're hoping to get some luck fishing from the pier, because you'll have to haul anything you can catch up through the air from the water. You will also need a reel with your rod and of course line and hooks, and there are many of the latter from which to choose. You will have to be advised about these too, and it's as well to remember that there are several different scales of hook sizes. Besides rod, reel, line and hooks you want some 'leads', which are weights which will keep your baited hook down near the sea bed. Then of course there are floats, so you will see that there are several things to buy. Perhaps you could borrow some tackle to see how you get on, or you could even try fishing with a baited line from a pier? A boy I know made his first rod from steel wireless aerials.

Now you must consider bait, and again it's wise to ask somebody who knows from experience what you will want for local fishing. It is possible sometimes to use artificial bait for certain fish but there's a lot of fun hunting for bait along the shore and in the rock-pools. Some of these baits are mentioned in my chapter on the sea-shore but I'll remind you about them again now.

There are two worms which can be dug from the sand which are generally used as bait for the fish that anglers called flatties—sole, plaice, flounders, brill and dabs. The first of these tasty baits is the LUGWORM and he's not at all easy to catch. I expect that as the tide goes down you have often seen on the smooth sand many tiny coils of damp sand rather like the cast of a worm in the garden at home. Look carefully and if you see plenty of little conical holes like funnels about a foot from each coil of sand you can be sure that there are plenty of lugworms under your feet. Each worm is in an underground tunnel about midway between his blow-hole and the little pile of sand thrown up from his burrow, and if you want to catch him you will have to dig quickly. Experts use a fork with broad prongs and dig between the funnel and the cast. The lugworm is not very far down in his U-shaped tunnel but he burrows very rapidly.

The RAGWORM is a very curious creature made up of a great many segments each of which carries a pair of bristly feet. He also has a fearsome-looking head armed with strong jaws and a pair of overlapping claws. He must be dug for, too, and only leaves a hole in the sand and no tell-tale cast. You can't mistake him because apart from his unusual appearance he is a pinkish colour with rainbow tints. Pick him up carefully because he can bite, but he makes very good bait.

The RAZOR-SHELL (which I also mention in the chapter on Shells) also make good bait and you must dig for them too. A blow-hole, bigger than that of the worm, gives away their hiding-place, and if you want to make sure that a razor-shell is at home tread down the sand firmly round the hole. If he is there, water will squirt out and you must then dig very fast to catch him because he is a quick burrower. These molluscs are about six inches long and you won't want many for a day's fishing as they can be cut up into small pieces for the hooks.

Other baits can be found in rock-pools and it's fun looking for them. All the following are mentioned elsewhere in this book —SHORE-CRABS, HERMIT-CRABS, LIMPETS, PRAWNS, SHRIMPS, COCKLES, for instance. Fish are cannibals and have no objection to eating other fish!

A good way to keep bait fresh—you'll probably be getting your bait one day ready for fishing the next—is to pack it between alternate layers of damp sand and seaweed in shoe boxes or the cardboard cartons any grocer will be pleased to give you.

Now it is time to tell you something about the fish you may be able to catch yourself, and a few others that are caught for you

The Lesser Black-Backed Gull is an aggressive, handsome bird, nearest in size to the herring-gull. Look for his bright yellow legs, and yellow and vermilion bill

Razor-Shells

Piddock

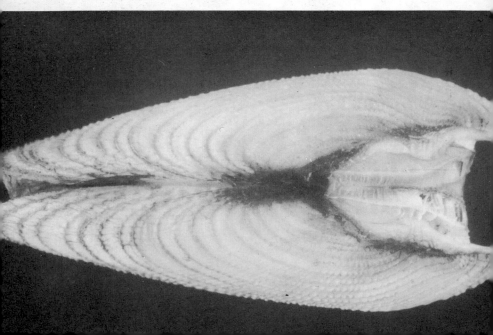

Of all our sea-birds, the Common Tern is the most fascinating and beautiful. He is slighter and smaller than his near relation, the gull, and his wings and tail are longer

Mussels

Oyster

Great Scallop

Cockles

The Arctic Tern is a summer visitor,
but it breeds in the north—mostly
in Scotland and Ireland

Common Periwinkles

Common Whelk

Lugworm

You will be lucky if you ever see the Little Tern, but it is a beauty. Under ten inches in length, it is the smallest of the tern family

and which you may see unloaded on the quays of some of our fishing ports when you are on holiday. Probably the most common of all the fish to be found in British waters is the popular HER-RING, but you have to be in the right place at the right time to see the exciting spectacle of the drifters racing into port to get the best possible price for their catches.

If you are in Scotland between June and August you may see the vessels come into Aberdeen, Fraserburgh or Peterhead, and if you are ever lucky enough to go to the Isle of Man in late summer you will see the Irish Sea herring fleets coming in to Peel. Fresh shoals arrive farther south down the east coast about the middle of August and I have seen the fleets landing their catches at Whitby and Scarborough in September. But the biggest herring harvest of all is brought into Great Yarmouth and Lowestoft in late autumn when you are back at school. The height of the season is usually around the full moon in October, although the fishermen never seem to be quite certain when the shoals will arrive, and sometimes the boats may be at sea for days without catching a single fish. The first sign of a shoal, which may be five miles broad and nine long, is often a crowd of screaming, fighting gulls swooping over the waves and then rising with squawks of triumph with glistening, silvery herrings in their cruel beaks. This must be an exciting moment for the fleet as the great drift-nets are dropped. As soon as the holds are full the drifters turn for home.

No doubt you remember that both kippers and bloaters are smoked herrings, and it is lucky for us that this tasty fish is so plentiful, for it is one of the cheapest and most nourishing of all sea-foods. Today we export herrings in various forms—both pickled and smoked—to some European countries. Although you are unlikely ever to catch a herring yourself I hope you'll see them landed one day.

A small relation of the herring is the PILCHARD. When it is about three inches long it is caught off the coasts of France under the name of sardine and comes to us packed tightly in olive-oil in a little tin box. Later in the season when it is full-grown to eight inches, 'schools' of pilchards move up to the south coasts of Devon and Cornwall. It is a pretty little fish with a rather heavy head for its size. Pilchard fleets go out from Newlyn, Looe and Mevagissey in the autumn and fish quite close to the coast using drift-nets. It seems that the best catches of pilchard are made during the hours of twilight so the boats do not go out until sunset. A pilchard lays up to 60,000 eggs about twenty miles out to sea, but it is odd that they are only to be found in such a comparatively small area round our south-western coasts. When next you go to Cornwall for a holiday in late summer look out for the pilchard fishing fleets.

It is time I told you about a fish that you can really catch yourself with very little trouble during the summer months. The MACKEREL is not only the most sporting and plucky fish in British waters but it is certainly the most handsome. When fully grown at about three years it is twelve inches long. No doubt you have often seen it on the fishmonger's slab, but when you first see it actually in the sea or when it has just been taken out you will be astonished at the brilliance of its gorgeous shining mail of blue and black, olive-green and silver. The back is criss-crossed with black, wavy bands.

The mackerel is another fish which cannot bear to live alone and large shoals visit our southern and western coasts as soon as the days become longer and warmer. Experts tell us that from the deep waters of the Atlantic out beyond Land's End they come in two great numberless streams—one up the Channel and the other up the Irish Sea. Again and again the shoals divide and sub-divide coming towards our shores to spawn and leaving again for deeper waters in early autumn. It is not surprising that the mackerel shoals could not be numbered even in millions because one female produces from 400,000 to 500,000 eggs which float at first and then, after a day or two, sink slowly to the bottom where they hatch out in the water.

The mackerel is a very fast swimmer and a great hunter, chasing every little sea creature within sight and darting through the water almost too fast for you to follow his movements.

All fishermen know when the mackerel shoals are coming in and it won't take you long to recognize the signs either. Mackerel feed mainly on shoals of tiny whitebait (a little fish about two and a half inches long) and as the latter tend to come into shallow water the mackerel follow them greedily. And not only the mackerel, for sea-birds—particularly gulls and terns—swoop down and attack them. So when you see hundreds of hungry birds wheeling, diving and screeching over the sea within sight of the shore you can be fairly certain of a shoal of mackerel.

There are several different ways of angling for this plucky fish and if I were you I should start by asking the advice of a local fisherman, going out with him in his boat and using a baited line with a lead. Mackerel will be tempted by lugworm, ragworm or a piece of fish flesh.

Now for the flat-fish or flatties—a large family, most of which are very good to eat and some of which you can certainly catch yourself. The best known are the soles, plaice, flounders, brill, dabs and the aristocratic turbot. There are several very odd characteristics of these flatties which live on the sea bottom. For instance they are *not born flat* but come from the egg the same shape as any other fish.

You will remember seeing, when you last enjoyed a flat-fish for dinner, that one side of it was white and the other had a dark skin which was probably covered with red spots. Perhaps you thought that the light surface was the front of the fish and the dark surface its back. However, although at first this seems ridiculous, the two surfaces are actually the two sides of the fish. The dark surface —the right side—is always uppermost and the light side is that on which the fish lies.

There is a good reason for the different colouring. The dark skin and coloured markings on the uppermost side of a flat-fish match the colour of the sea bottom and make it almost invisible. If it ever rested light side up, it would be easily found by its enemies. Actually, nearly all the fish seem to have the gift of adapting their colour to suit the background against which they live, but, if you can ever visit an aquarium, you will see how difficult it is to distinguish a plaice against the sandy bottom of its tank.

Another odd thing about the flat-fish is that instead of having an eye on each side of its head it has two eyes on the same side— the upper side, of course—and this is stranger still when we remember that the flat-fish is born with one eye *each* side of its head like any other fish. It swims upright, as do other fish also, but when it is about three weeks old it leaves the shallower water near the shore, gently sinks to the bottom of the sea, and tends to topple over towards the left. After a little it flattens out, with one eye gazing upwards through the water but the other, of course, close to the sandy bottom of the sea. About this time the shape of the fish's head begins to change, and, what is even more remarkable, *the left eye begins to travel round the head*, away from the position in which it cannot possibly be of any use, until it is in line with the right one. The left eye makes the journey round the head in fifteen days, and by this time the appearance and swimming habits of the fish have completely changed. Its short-lived power of lovely, darting flight through the sea has now gone, and it has become a sluggish flat-fish, seemingly content to lie for ever on its left side, which now loses all its colour.

Now let me tell you something about the best known of these strange creatures of the sea bottom.

First the PLAICE, which is the best known of the flat-fish, and the most valuable to us as food. Some of them are a foot or more long, and a few which have been caught have actually weighed fourteen pounds. Incredible though it seems, the female plaice produces between a quarter- and a half-million eggs, although this is a considerably smaller number than that of some of its near relatives such as the turbot. It is easily recognized by the large red spots on the upper side of the body, and is likely to be caught where there is plenty of sand and gravel on the sea bottom. Plaice can be caught with a rod and line on a bait of lugworms and ragworms or small pieces of fish flesh. The best fishing is from a boat.

Although the plaice is the most important flat-fish to the British fish trade the COMMON SOLE is the most expensive, and is considered to be the best flavoured of all sea-fish. It is livelier than the plaice, has a more flexible body, and escapes more easily through the meshes of a net which will hold other fish of the same size. It seems to prefer darkness to light, and is more easily caught at night-time. In shape it is almost oval, and its upper side is a brownish grey with darker splodges of brown. The LEMON-SOLE is generally smaller than the common sole and an almost perfect oval in shape. In colour it is a rich brownish yellow, marked with darker- and lighter-coloured spots. The head is very small but, like the plaice, it has the same curiously lop-sided mouth.

The FLOUNDER flourishes in salt, brackish and even fresh water, preferring patches of mud and sand, say at the mouth of an estuary. It is brown with some darker patches merging into black and the underside is a beautiful pearly white. You cannot mistake it for a plaice because it has no spots of red or orange and the 'wrist' to the tail is longer and more slender. It is greedy for lugworms and ragworms.

The little DAB is the smallest of the flat-fish and one you might easily catch from a boat near the shore or from the pier. Baby dabs, only an inch or so in size, can easily be caught close inshore with a shrimping-net in August and September, particularly on the west coast. It is sandy brown in colour and loves sandy, shallow bays.

The magnificent TURBOT is sometimes called 'the king of sea-fish', and there are some who also think it is the finest-flavoured.

Specimens have been caught up to a weight of forty pounds and up to three feet in length. It does not like our northern waters very much, but trawlers off our west coast and in the English Channel do very well with it. As the female can produce from *five to ten million eggs*, there should be all the turbot we can eat in our own seas, although it prefers shallow waters. It has a diamond-shaped body of speckled brown colouring.

Like the turbot, the BRILL has an equal-sided mouth but it is narrower in its proportion to its length, and has usually some whitish spots on its brown skin. It lives almost entirely on other fish and is common all round the British Isles.

There are other flat-fish in British waters, of course. There is, for instance, the enormous halibut which sometimes can reach a size of five feet, but this breeds in deep northern waters, and there is also the ugly skate, but you are not very likely to see either of them.

Another well-known family of fish is the cod, to which is related the haddock, the whiting and the POLLACK. I must tell you something about the latter because you might see some caught off rocky parts of the coast and they are fairly common. It's a handsome fish, especially when just caught, for then its brilliant colouring of bronze and olive-green shines like polished armour. The belly is yellowish white and it can be recognized by its jutting lower jaw. The average weight is four pounds although they can be much heavier. Fishing for pollack is exciting and they can be caught either from the rocks themselves or from a boat fairly close inshore. They are sporting fish and there are many ways of catching them.

There's not much to tell you about the WHITING. No doubt you've often eaten it and you're more likely to see it caught in winter than in summer. They are small fish, averaging not much more than one pound in weight, coloured silver with a sheen of gold. Young whiting are often found in shallow water close inshore in sandy bays and estuaries. They are particularly fond of young shrimps as a meal and consequently many thousands are caught and destroyed in shrimping nets before they can grow into a fish big enough to be eaten. Experienced anglers agree that evening is the best time to fish for whiting because the shoals move into shallow water as soon as it gets dark.

There are many other fish that I have not mentioned here because if you become keen on sea-fishing you'll want a much bigger book about them than this. I have told you, however, about some of those fish you might catch yourself or watch being caught by your father or other grown-ups from the rocks, the pier, the shore or from a boat. Even if you go to the seaside for a day in winter or spring you will still find men fishing. There must be something worth while in such a sport and perhaps I've told you enough to start you off. I hope so.

5

Sea-Birds

Of all living creatures birds are the most vital and joyously alive. It is impossible to imagine the countryside without them, but I've often thought that we notice birds more at the seaside than we do inland. Perhaps this is because most of them are bigger than those seen in our gardens, woods and hedgerows, but I am sure that the seaside will mean more to you if you learn to recognize many of the lovely birds that breed and build their nests on our cliffs and haunt our shores.

You will learn most about sea-birds, of course, if you are able to go to the seaside at their breeding time early in the year, for even then the ocean-going kinds must, just for a while, desert the sea for land. But whenever or wherever you go to the coast you will be thrilled with the sea-birds if you are patient and clever enough to watch them carefully at rest or in flight.

ONE OF THE greatest marvels of nature is the migration of birds as they fly across land and sea from one country to another and sometimes even from one continent to another. And to me it has always seemed almost as remarkable that many frail-looking sea-birds such as the swallow-like terns are often seen so far from land. Only once a year do some of these birds find their way back across thousands of miles of trackless, heaving water to their breeding places on some distant shore. Through storms and fog they fight their way and nobody yet knows what physical power or instinct guides them so correctly to the lonely islands and coasts where you could see them during the earlier part of each year if you could go exploring then.

There is another rather odd thing about sea-birds. Have you ever realized that their calls are not as melodious as those of their inland relations? When you have time and opportunity to recognize their voices, however, you will find a strange and haunting beauty in their wind-tossed cries.

Many of our rarest birds breed only on our lonely northern shores. Sometimes, in severe winters, such beautiful, graceful birds as the wild geese come south. A few miles from where I live in Sussex is a shallow valley down which runs a muddy river. As it nears the sea it finds its way through a gap in the high chalk cliffs and then runs free over the shingle. To this valley of the Cuckmere occasionally come birds rarely seen in the more kindly south, and some of us have watched with wonder and admiration a 'V' of geese sailing over the South Downs towards the shelter of this haven.

I remember once reading a poem which suggested that the spirits of old seamen live on in the gulls which are perhaps the most competent and adaptable of all birds. Although they are sea-birds, they are sometimes seen inland on the farmers' fields, where they do much good by eating pests in the soil, and they are now well known in London. All Londoners love the gulls, which come screaming and tumbling up the muddy tidewater of the Thames and clamour for titbits round the bridges and barges.

Sailors say that gulls cry loudly round dangerous rocks and cliffs in a fog, and fishermen claim that they lead them unerringly to the herring shoals. There are various types all round our coasts, and I expect a gull will be the first sea-bird you will recognize, as he glides gracefully with wings widespread down from the clifftop and then swoops over the water. Sometimes you will see him riding on the waves a few yards from the shore, but if he thinks you have something for him to eat, he will wheel round and round you until you toss a titbit into the air for him. If he comes near enough you will notice his rather cruel, hooked beak, which enables him to tear at his food like an eagle. Gulls are magnificent scavengers, and help to keep our beaches clean.

There are at least fifty members of this fascinating family to be found round our shores, and here are some notes to help you to recognize some of them, but they are not easy to identify. Perhaps the most important points to look for are the colour of the legs and the shape and pattern of the wing-tips. Some gulls change the colour of their plumage several times between their first year of life and maturity.

First then let me introduce you to the HERRING-GULL which is the commonest of the gulls, and can be found nearly everywhere at the seaside and sometimes inland too on lakes and reservoirs.

He is a very lovely bird, with grey and white plumage, black wing-tips, pink legs, and a yellow bill with a red spot on it, but I think you will recognize him first by his incomparable gift of flight. No other winged creature can glide in the teeth of the wind as he can, and some naturalists say that no other bird has such a wonderful mastery of the air. Many birds can outfly this gull, but no other English bird is such a beautiful glider or uses currents of air so skilfully to save his strength.

All sea-travellers know the herring-gull, for he follows ocean liners for many miles with scarcely a beat of his wings. Although he is such a joy to watch, his voice is ugly and his manners deplorable. If ever you see fish being unloaded from trawlers on the quayside, you will be almost deafened by the raucous scream-ing of the herring-gulls as they pounce on fish-heads or offal.

In the spring these gulls gather into colonies and build their nests on the ledges or grassy slopes of cliffs. The nest is quite elaborately made of grass and seaweed and other strange oddments picked up round the high-tide mark. Some herring-gulls have been known to decorate their nests with wild flowers.

Three olive-tinted eggs with brown and black blotches are laid in May, but the fledglings remain mottled brown in colour until the third or fourth year of their lives, when they put on the lovely grey and white plumage of their parents. Here, however, is a guide to their changes of plumage and appearance. During the first year, apart from their speckled brown feathers, the tips of the tail feathers are black. The bill is a brownish yellow and the legs black. There's not much change during the second year and although the tail seems to be a little lighter it still has its black tip. By the third year the herring-gull has virtually grown up and, although there may still be a few traces of brown on the upper sides of the wings and tail, the cruel bill is now yellow with its familiar scarlet spot, while the legs and feet are a brownish pink.

A foolishly named member of this noisy family is the BLACK-HEADED GULL. This is the smallest of the gulls and it is mis-named because in winter the head is white! By the end of February, however, the head appears to be covered with a brownish 'hood' and this is worn all through the summer. They are not really sea-gulls at all because, although you may sometimes see them on the coast, you are just as likely to see them in big towns and cities. Londoners know them well, for not only are they busy in the parks during the winter, but they are always flying over the Victoria Embankment and sailing and wheeling across the muddy river Thames. You will also see this gull in the country, following the plough as it turns over the soil in brown furrows when the days are short. The farmer welcomes the black-headed gulls for they gobble up grubs and harmful insects and save him a lot of trouble. They're quite easy to recognize—first by their size which is only about fifteen inches from beak to the tip of the tail, and secondly by their deep red bills and legs and the white edge on the front of the wings. The breeding season is between April and June when they leave the towns and congregate in enormous colonies on sand dunes near the sea, on marshy land and sometimes by inland reservoirs. There are generally three eggs in a nest of sticks and grass. Oddly enough the colour of the eggs seems to vary from bluish green to olive or buff blotched with dark brown.

The black-headed gull's cry is an ugly scream. In flight over the breeding-ground in spring they are a wonderful sight.

The GREAT BLACK-BACKED GULL is the largest member of the gull family with a wing-span of sometimes nearly six feet. He is not often seen in the south and west of Britain though he is commoner in Scotland and on the rocky islands off that part of our coasts. I have seen them at Lowestoft and at Whitby farther north when the herring fleets come in and they fight and scream for fish offal as the herrings are gutted on the quays.

Adults of both sexes are easier to recognize in the summer. Apart from their size, the head and neck are white, the back and wings dark grey with white tips. The tail is white, the cruel beak pale yellow, with a scarlet patch on the lower mandible, and the legs and feet a pale flesh-colour.

The flight of this gull is very graceful and strong, and although his dark grey mantle is very like that of his near relation, the lesser black-backed gull, you can tell the difference between them by their size and the colour of their legs. The lesser has yellow legs.

Although he is handsome to look at, this big sea-bird has very unpleasant habits, for he is a greedy, merciless killer, and often kills when he is not even hungry. Strangely enough, he is a clumsy killer too, and there is a horrid savagery about the way in which he will attack smaller sea-birds such as puffins, shearwaters and terns, and, having killed them, leave their bodies on the rocks. Sometimes you will see him strutting along the beach as if he were 'king of the castle', but although he may look almost harmless, he is in reality a bold, bad pirate.

These gulls nest in colonies on a rocky island or cliff-edge. The nest is a tangle of seaweed and grass, and three eggs are usually laid. It takes four years for the fledgling to grow into a mature gull in all his handsome plumage.

The LESSER BLACK-BACKED GULL is a jaunty, good-looking bird which is nearest in size to the herring-gull. Most of his plumage is a lovely white, but the wing-tips are black with white 'mirrors'; the back, of course, is black and, as I have already told you, the legs are bright yellow. Look too for his yellow and vermilion bill.

There are big colonies of these gulls in Devon, Cornwall, along the Welsh coast, and in Scotland and Ireland, and usually this gull prefers marshland or quiet inlets and estuaries to cliffs. Sometimes he can be seen quite a long way inland, though his principal diet is small fish and sea-animals, and other sea-birds, but he likes the eggs and sometimes attacks and kills the fledglings of sea-birds, particularly puffins and shearwaters. He is a scavenger, too, which is in his favour, for he does a lot to keep our harbours and beaches clear of carrion.

Except for his lovely plumage, which sometimes takes four years to grow, he is not a very pleasant neighbour because he is so rarely seen and too much heard. His cry is ugly and unmistakable—*owk-owk*, running together to make a peal of eerie laughter.

He usually nests in colonies and quite often on the coast as well as inland, on moors or by lakes. There are generally three eggs which may vary a lot in colour and the type of nest varies too—sometimes it's only a scrape in the ground and sometimes quite a pile of rubbish. Gulls have very odd habits. Although handsome enough this one is a ruthless robber and killer.

Another member of this big family is the COMMON GULL, which is also misnamed because it is not at all 'common'. Sometimes it is called the seamew, and although it can be seen in Kent where a colony was founded some years ago, it is less rare in Scotland where it nests freely on grassy slopes near the coast and sometimes in fresh-water lochs during May and June. The nest is made of grass and dried seaweed and the eggs, usually three in number, vary in colour but are usually dark olive, blotched with dark brown.

In early autumn large numbers of the common gulls come to our east coast from Germany, Holland, Norway and Denmark to winter in our islands. Inland they sometimes follow the plough and are a great help to the farmer.

This gull is a little larger than its black-headed relation but smaller than the herring-gull. When fully grown the bill is greenish yellow and much smaller and more slender than the latter's. The legs and feet are a greenish yellow also, and quite unmistakable.

Of the same family as the noisy, greedy gulls already mentioned is the gentler, pretty KITTIWAKE, which is usually found only on our north and west coasts, nesting in great colonies on the dizzy precipices of our highest cliffs. It is named after its haunting and plaintive cry—*kittiway-eek, kittiway-eek*—which cannot possibly be mistaken for that of any other bird.

In appearance it is rather like the black-headed gull, without the black head, but its back is a lovely pearly grey, the legs nearly black, and the bill greenish yellow. The wing-tips are solid black. Immature birds are barred with brown. The kittiwake is most graceful in all its movements and compared with the other gulls has a dark and kindly eye.

Kittiwakes are great travellers and spend the winter on the open sea, where they are continually exposed to the full fury of the Atlantic gales. When the storms are very bad the small fish upon which they feed are driven deeper under the waves—too deep for the little kittiwake to reach by diving—and so many thousands of these beautiful little gulls perish of starvation. Incidentally, it is the only one of the commoner gulls which dives and swims under water for fish.

It is the kittiwake which follows the ocean liners right across the Atlantic, and although it looks so small and frail, it can out-fly many of its bigger relations.

In April and May the kittiwakes come back to the nesting-places on the cliffs, and here, if you are lucky, you will see them courting in a charming manner. The chicks are hatched later than those of the other gulls and are deserted by their parents in August. You are not likely ever to see a kittiwake's nest, for it builds on rock ledges far out of reach of humans, but all through the nesting season these charming birds are a delight to watch. The two or three eggs are usually pale buff or grey, blotched with brown round the larger end. Each parent pair is so obviously devoted that they share the domestic duties of raising a family, and even feed each other. And when one is absent for a while they call to each other, *kittiway-eek, kittiway-eek,* as if their hearts were broken.

Another beautiful sea-bird is the COMMON TERN, sometimes called the sea-swallow, but this is not a very good name, as we think of a swallow choosing the haunts of men for its home, whereas the tern is a true gipsy and only visits our coasts, where it nests in tremendous colonies.

Perhaps of all our sea-birds the tern is the most fascinating and beautiful. He is slighter and smaller than his near relation, the gull. The plumage is white, the wings pearl-grey, the bill red with a black tip, the head wears a jaunty little black cap and his lovely body is supported by coral-red legs. You will soon learn the difference between a tern and a gull when you see the tern's longer wings and longer tail. His tail is also deeply forked.

The tern uses his wings almost lazily, and sometimes you may watch him drifting and gliding aimlessly for hours over tidal waters, until he drops like a stone to the surface and then, if his luck holds, rises with a fish in his beak.

The terns come to us in April from the warmer south. They sometimes return to their old nesting-places, but not always, and nobody has been able to explain such fickleness, for some of the tern colonies are tremendous. Occasionally they build among rocks, but more often they choose sand dunes or flat coastal country. Their nests are extraordinary, for some birds take the trouble to build them of woven grass or seaweed, others use seaweed and shells, while some are content with a scrape in the ground. Sometimes the nests are built so close together that it is impossible not to tread on them, and the eggs when laid differ in shape, size and colouring. Some terns put stones in the nest beside the eggs.

Terns are very good colonizers, and will rise to attack any of the bigger gulls which have the temerity to come too near the ternery. But they have one strange and unaccountable habit which nobody has been able to explain. Sometimes during the nesting season, when the ground is white with the bodies of tens of thousands of brooding terns, a sudden hush falls on the ternery and then, as if at some secret signal, the whole body of birds rises into the air and moves in a compact cloud out to sea. Some have said that these strange and sudden flights are through fear or panic, but it is odd that every adult bird should become so fearful that it is prepared to desert eggs or chicks, which will most certainly be snapped up by cruel and hungry neighbours. We know that the tern is brave enough upon occasions in defence of its young, so these sudden desertions are all the more remarkable.

Mr. R. M. Lockley, whose books I hope you will read if you are fond of birds, has been studying such strange habits as these for many years. He suggests that fear cannot be the only motive, and that there is always *one* bird which may be a leader or may just be the bird which happens to be in front and leads the way. Naturalists are certain, however, that this strange movement, which always seems to be the answer to an unknown summons, is more of a ritual than anything else and is not caused by disturbance or panic. Migration to the south starts again in September, but I hope that you will see the lovely terns before they go.

There are three other terns you might see, but they are not very common. The ARCTIC TERN is another summer visitor, but it breeds in the north—mostly in Scotland and Ireland. The bill and legs are red.

The largest member of this family is the SANDWICH TERN which has black legs and a black beak with a yellow tip. Its white forked tail has shorter streamers than those of the other terns.

You will be lucky if you ever see the LITTLE TERN, but it is a beauty. Under ten inches in length, it is the smallest of the family. It has yellow legs, a yellow bill with a black tip and, like the other terns, it is fitted with a black cap—but a cap with a difference, for it is broken with a white forehead. The small nesting colonies are usually on sandy flats but I have never been lucky enough to see one.

The terns are not as common as the gulls, but you cannot possibly mistake a ternery and they are all most beautiful birds in flight.

Now for some larger birds. The auks are not as common as the gulls and terns but well worth looking out for. The members of this family are really ocean and not coast birds. They live on fish for which they dive and swim under water, but they breed and raise their chicks on the most precipitous cliffs they can find.

46

And here is a special warning. Never go too close to the edge of a cliff, and even from the beach do not try to climb up either for fun or in search of birds' nests and eggs. It's silly and selfish to risk your life and the lives of others who may have to rescue you. Try to get as much fun as you can by just *watching* birds and so learning to know them. Please remember this. People who live near the coast as I do know these dangers.

But to return to the auks. If you are near a rocky part of the coast you may see them in May but, sad to say, because they are ocean-swimmers you may sometimes find their bodies washed up on the shore with their feathers clogged by the foul, black oil-waste which so often messes our beaches and tortures and kills so many beautiful sea-birds.

The first of these big birds is the GUILLEMOT (about eighteen inches long when full-grown). I have never seen one on my part of the south coast, but they may be found in the breeding season congregating in uncountable multitudes on Flamborough Head, the Bempton Cliffs, the Bass Rock and the Farne Islands. Only one egg is laid, and no egg ever had a harder bed, for it lies on a tiny patch of bare rock hundreds of feet above the sea. The guillemot's egg is pear-shaped and long, so that it does not roll into the sea. No two guillemots' eggs ever seem to be the same colour or to have similar markings, and they may be any shade of brown, green, yellow or nearly white, with or without blotches or lines of brown. The guillemot is white-breasted and wears a mouse-coloured livery. In winter some white appears on cheeks and throat. His feet are webbed, and he is a magnificent diver and swims under the water *with his wings*. He is extraordinarily affectionate and intelligent, as has been proved by those who have rescued and cleansed a living bird of oil, and kept it for a while as a pet. The call seems to be a peculiar grunt.

Next comes the RAZOR-BILL, which is very like the guillemot, but his plumage is black with white underparts and a white bar on the wing, and he also has a great, thick, black bill. His face and throat turn white in winter, and when he is swimming you'll notice his pointed tail cocked up. Razor-bills usually breed with guillemots on the ledges of high cliffs. The razor-bill is a very fast flier.

The third member of the auk family about which I want to tell you is the odd-looking PUFFIN, sometimes called the sea-parrot. This is a bird you cannot possibly mistake. It is quite common on our western coasts. He is very thick-set with white underparts and cheeks, while the plumage of the upper parts is nearly black. He also has a neat black collar. The short legs and webbed feet are scarlet or orange, but it is his massive bill, like that of a parrot, which is most remarkable: no other sea-bird has one like this, for it is striped with blue, scarlet and yellow.

The puffin is a plump and serious-looking bird and, rather like the penguin, seems oddly 'un-bird-like'. His eye, circled with crimson, seems to regard the world with some bewilderment, and we cannot help feeling that he is rather a pathetic little creature. On land he is somewhat helpless, and provides many a good meal for a prowling gull; but if he cannot take care of himself he certainly does his best to safeguard his single egg, which is laid in a burrow or tunnel on a cliff-top. The puffin colonies are very crowded, and there are so many burrows that it is hardly safe to walk over the surface of the turf. It must be a very strange experience for a baby puffin, born underground, to be hustled out into the daylight and then rudely given a first flying lesson! The puffin lives on fish for which it dives and swims under water.

Those are the three most important members of the auk family and I want now to tell you about three fine fishers. The first and most spectacular is the magnificent GANNET—a powerful, handsome sea-hawk with a wing-span of nearly six feet. His plumage is white with big, black tips on the long, narrow wings. Like a hawk, which can see a mouse move in the grass far below him, so can the gannet see a fish just below the surface of the waves and drop like an arrow into the water for his meal. It is said that there are only fifteen breeding-places of the gannet in the world, and that eleven of these are round our coasts. The most famous of these is the Bass Rock off the North Berwick coast, where in the breeding season the precipitous black crags are white with gannets jostling each other on the rock ledges. Each nest, to which the birds return every year, is built quite high with seaweed, turf and other fragments of flotsam that the bird can find.

The gannet has been well described as 'the kingfisher of the sea', and it is true that he has an amazing skill in catching fish. I only hope that you are lucky enough one day to see his spectacular dive which may be from a height of a hundred feet. When he drops towards the waves remember that he takes a high dive because he knows that the momentum will give him speed *under* the water. A fraction of a second before he strikes the water he closes his wings and then opens them slightly to act as a brake when he is under. He generally swallows the fish he has caught before coming to the surface, and I should think that this is because he is afraid

Of the same family as the gulls, the gentler, pretty Kittiwakes are usually found only on our north and west coasts, nesting in great colonies on the dizzy precipices of our highest cliffs

Trawler

Deep-sea trawling off Iceland

Pilchard boat

Herring boat

You cannot possibly mistake these odd-looking Puffins, members of the auk family. It is their massive bill, like that of a parrot, which is most remarkable, for it is striped with blue, scarlet and yellow

his meal may be snatched by another bird—you remember the habits of the gulls, don't you?

The gannet has another strange habit, for instead of sitting on the single big egg and brooding over it with her body, she uses her feet, placed one over the other on top of the egg. The egg is hatched by this strange means after six and a half weeks, and the chick remains for two more months in the nest. Like the shearwater and other petrels, the gannets desert their young, so that the chicks are forced to fend for themselves, and get ready to brave the wide wastes of the ocean by jumping over the edge of the cliff!

The CORMORANT is not of the same family as the gannet but he is a wonderful fisher, and you're much more likely to see him for he's fairly common. The best specimens I've ever seen were on the west coast of Scotland, but he can often be seen on estuaries and tidal rivers and occasionally on inland waters. You may see him fishing for eels, of which he is particularly fond. He is rather an untidy-looking bird, with black or very dark brown plumage, with a sheen of purple or green on the feathers, and a white chin. He does not do a high dive like the gannet, but swims on the surface of the sea and then suddenly somersaults forward and grabs a fish under water. He is a very good swimmer, particularly under water, when he uses his big webbed feet to advantage. When on the surface he is rather low in the water with his neck upright and beak tilted up a little. He is a big bird, up to three feet high. Occasionally he has been known to build a nest of sticks and grass inland, even in a tree, but this is very rare. The nest is usually made of seaweed on rocky cliffs and islands. If you can watch him on his untidy nest, you will see his shaggy, rough-feathered neck shining with a darker gleam than the rest of his feathers; and by this 'collar' you will be able to know and remember him. Another characteristic is that he perches upright on a rock or post with wings half-open.

A close but smaller relation to the odd-looking cormorant is the SHAG which has no white markings on the head. In spring, at breeding time, it wears a crest on the head, but it is almost entirely a bird of the wild, rocky cliffs and tiny islands off the west coast. I remember going on a steamer trip from Oban in Scotland round the islands of Iona, Staffa and Mull on a very rough day, and it was then that I saw shags for the first and only time.

Now for some smaller birds—the fascinating family of petrels. The best known of these are the STORMY PETRELS, sometimes known as Mother Carey's Chickens and referred to as such in

Charles Kingsley's famous book, *The Water Babies*. It is said that sailors still use this name because the appearance of the stormy petrels near a ship is supposed to foretell bad weather.

Unless you visit the Scilly Islands or the lonely little islands off the Scottish, Irish or south Welsh coasts in May or June, you are not likely to see the stormy petrel, for it lives at sea after hatching its single egg. It is the smallest of the British sea-birds, being no bigger than a chaffinch, and yet it will be seen far out in the Atlantic, following in the wake of big ships—tossing and dipping like a butterfly and then skimming low over the water with dangling legs. It was this unusual habit of 'paddling', or walking on the waves, that helped it to get its name, for 'petrel' is derived from Saint Peter, who had faith enough to walk on the waves when he was bidden to do so by his Master.

The adult bird is sooty black, with a square tail splashed with white, and a white rump. The legs and webbed feet are black, too, and it is fairly easy to recognize.

Mr. R. M. Lockley, whom I mentioned earlier in this chapter, lived for a time on the island of Skokholm, off the coast of Pembrokeshire, and made a great study of the petrels and shearwaters which came to the neighbouring islands in April to breed. He has many fascinating stories to tell of them. In the breeding season the petrels are never seen in the day-time, but are very active and quite noisy at night. The single egg, like that of the puffin, is laid underground in a rabbit-hole or burrow, but Mr. Lockley believes that the birds 'lie low' in day-time, because they would most certainly be persecuted by gulls, hawks and crows if they were seen using the burrow. As soon as it is dark, however, the little petrels set up a strange purring sound and become very restless. The male and female birds take it in turns to sit on the egg while the other is away at sea, and sometimes a spell of duty has been known to last three days. All the birds of this family feed far out in the ocean.

The MANX SHEARWATER is another, bigger member of the petrel family, and like the stormy petrel it feeds at sea, breeds on a few lonely islands off the west coast, and flies far afield at night. It is as large as a pigeon, with a sooty back, white underparts, and a strong hooked beak. This shearwater is able to dig its own burrow at nesting-time and, like the swallow, it often comes back to this same burrow early every spring and meets its own mate again. Puffins or a rabbit may have taken charge of the burrow, but the shearwater is able to give a rabbit a good nip with its beak, though a puffin may be too strong to be evicted. The shearwaters take seven and a half weeks to hatch their single white egg, sharing the duty, and then the chick stays in the nest for another ten and a half weeks. Unlike the stormy petrel, the manx shearwater does not follow ships.

The FULMAR is also an ocean bird and a member of the same family. You will not often see it, because it breeds in the north, but the plumage is white with a grey mantle and tail, and there are few other sea-birds with so perfect a flight. Like the shearwater, it loves to sport among the troughs and crests of the waves, and its command of the air makes even the flight of a gull look slow and clumsy. Whereas other birds use their wings as pinions, the fulmar never seems to beat the air, but rather to use every wind current to make its lovely, graceful flight look effortless. It lays only one white egg in May on a rocky ledge or in a little hollow in the turf.

There are many other lovely sea-birds that I could tell you about and I realize that I've told you about many which you may never see, because you may not visit the part of our coasts where they breed and live. Don't be disheartened if on your next seaside holiday you only recognize a few of those I have described. If you watch carefully you'll soon begin to recognize them. It is not easy to know all the gulls because their plumage changes as they get older, neither is it simple to tell the difference between sea- and shore-birds, but you will probably remember now that there are ocean-dwellers like the high-diving gannets, the lovely petrels and the shearwaters. Others like the gulls are always to be seen round our shores through the year, and I haven't got room to tell you about the ducks and geese which use the estuaries and mud flats. Many that I have told you about are migrants, coming to us from other shores to breed, and then leaving us after a few months, but the most fascinating thing about all birds is, I think, that they have such different habits and characteristics. Many people today spend a lifetime studying them and admiring their grace and beauty. I hope you will get a lot of fun out of watching them at the seaside.

6

Guardians of Our Coasts

The coasts of Britain are guarded night and day. The coast-guard watches the ships that pass, and as dusk falls the beacons of the light-houses and lightships flash their warning. Sometimes when the clammy fog slips in from the sea and hides the rocks and sand-banks and when no light can be seen through the gloom, the guardians of our coasts send out on fog-horns and sirens their warning to the groping ships. Since the war, of course, wireless signals and radar, too, are used to guide the sailors of all nations as they enter our waters.

And always at the alert and ready to help are the brave crews who man the life-boats and who go out in all weathers at the risk of their lives to save those in peril on the sea.

THE PURPOSE OF all the coastal lights, of the Coast-Guard Service and, of course, of the life-boat crews is *to save life*. I told you in the first chapter that the sea is a hard, cruel and treacherous master. All sailors know that it must never be trifled with and that man cannot tame it. They know too that round our coasts there are always men watching over them and their ships, ready to guide them into safe waters.

The warning lights which are the lighthouse and lightship services are controlled by a remarkable organization in London called Trinity House. The coast-guards are managed by the Ministry of Transport and the life-boats maintained by the Royal National Life-Boat Institution—a typically British service which is *voluntary*. Many books have been written about the life-boats so I am not going to tell you much about them, except to stress one important thing. Except for a comparatively few people who are quite rightly paid for their full-time duties, the service as a whole is run by those who give their time of their own free will. This giving of time and money to keep the life-boats ready to save life is a great credit to us and an example which has now been followed by many other countries.

Let me tell you first something about the lights. A map big enough to show the towns round our coasts will help to make this chapter more interesting.

It has always seemed fitting to me that Trinity House should be on Tower Hill overlooking the Thames, the historic Tower of London and the Tower Bridge. It is indeed part of history. In the reign of Henry VII some pilots and sailors living in a place called Deptford Strond in Kent formed themselves into a guild. I expect you have heard that the guilds in the Middle Ages were societies of men following the same craft or calling. There would, for instance, be a guild of stone-masons, or weavers or tanners. Usually these guilds were dedicated to the honour of a saint, for in those days it was clearly understood that the skill to do good work was a gift from God, and that all work should be done in His name. The pilots and coast-watchers of Deptford Strond therefore dedicated their guild to the honour of the Holy Trinity for the purpose of 'watching over the interests of all concerned with shipping'. Henry VIII in 1514 incorporated 'the guild fraternity or brotherhood of the most glorious and undivided Trinity and of St. Clement in the parish of Deptford in the County of Kent commonly called the Corporation of Trinity House of Deptford Strond'. Queen Elizabeth I gave the corporation the absolute and sole right of putting up beacons round our coasts. Today, with a few exceptions, such as Liverpool Bay and the Mersey, Trinity House looks after all the lighthouses of England and Wales. The money to pay for the lighthouses and lightships comes from 'light dues', which are charged on all ships using any of the ports of the United Kingdom.

I cannot tell you now about all the lighthouses round our coasts, but I hope you will have the chance of seeing at least a few of those I will describe. When you are on holiday you should visit the nearest lighthouse and see whether there is a chance of looking over it. The public are sometimes admitted to certain lighthouses, and I have been over several including St. Catherine's in the Isle of Wight, the old Dungeness light and that at Hartland Point on the north Devon coast.

Most of the warning beacons are from oil-burning lamps with wonderful reflectors, but some are electric from current generated in the lighthouse itself. Sailors know that different lighthouses have different sorts of beams flashing at varying intervals. Not all the lights are white, but all seamen know which is which and so are able to check their position after dark in any weather except dense fog.

The most dangerous approach to our shores is probably that coming in from the Atlantic up the Channel to Plymouth or up the Bristol Channel. The first British lighthouse you would see on such a voyage would be the famous BISHOP ROCK standing on a rock four miles west of the Scilly Islands. This is a terrible place in a storm for it is exposed to the full fury of the Atlantic gales, and it is little wonder that the tower took seven years to build as it was only possible to work on it when the weather was calm. The lantern, which shows a powerful double-flashing light, is 146 feet above the level of high tide. It is said that no other lighthouse in the world stands in such an exposed position.

Sailing east towards Plymouth, the next light you would see would be the WOLF ROCK which is the third most important lighthouse round this part of the coast. It is about eight miles from Land's End, and is so called because the rocks upon which it is built used to give out a growling sound as the waves rushed into a hollow part of them. For many years it was believed to be impossible to build a lighthouse on the Wolf because of the swirl of the currents and the force of the surf. In 1860, however, Trinity House began work on the present tower, but it took nine years to finish.

There is another light actually on land at the LIZARD but the next, the EDDYSTONE, is certainly one of the most important in the world. The rock after which it is named stands up in the English Channel, in the track of all shipping, about fourteen miles from Plymouth and about nine miles from the Cornish coast. Before the first lighthouse was built—the present building is the fourth—this reef of rocks, which is almost entirely covered at high tide, was the cause of many terrible wrecks. The flashing light of Eddystone can be seen seventeen miles away, and it has been flashing every night now since May 1882. The building before this present one was a remarkable tribute to its makers. It stood for a century and might well be standing now if the rock on which it was built had not become undermined. The 'stump' of the old lighthouse still stands near the new tower.

Steaming up-channel towards the Straits of Dover, the most important lighthouses you would see are the two on the Devon coast at START POINT and BERRY HEAD. Then there are two more important and familiar lights on the Isle of Wight. The first is the NEEDLES, marking the western entrance to the Solent, which is the channel between the island and the mainland. The jagged pinnacles of chalk here are very dangerous. The other is ST. CATHERINE'S on the southernmost point of the island.

On our voyage down the English Channel we pass the mighty chalk cliffs of BEACHY HEAD, by Eastbourne. These cliffs are where the South Downs run into the sea and are an obvious place for a lighthouse. But if you look up you see the cliff-top is bare, and you must look down at the base of the cliff to find the warning light. The first lighthouse here *was* built on the cliff, but was not a success, as its light was often hidden by the severe fogs which at certain times of the year slide up the Channel. In 1902, therefore, a new tower was built on the foreshore five hundred feet away from the foot of the cliffs for, strangely enough, the mists which so often shrouded the heights were not seen at sea-level. It would have been a great thrill to watch this new lighthouse being built, for all the materials were brought down from the top of the cliffs by cable railway.

We next pass the great dreary bank of shingle called Dungeness at the eastern end of Rye Bay. This was a particularly dangerous place in the days of sailing ships and was called a 'graveyard full of sailors' bones'. The point of the Ness grows farther out to sea every year, and it became essential to build a magnificent new lighthouse nearer the sea. This is the first new lighthouse built for many years and it is very striking, with two black and two white bands on the 120-foot concrete tower. It was officially opened by the Duke of Gloucester on 29 June 1960, and if you are ever in Kent or east Sussex you should go and see it. You could combine this trip with a ride on the Romney, Hythe and Dymchurch miniature railway which will take you to the lighthouse from Hythe.

The last promontory on the Channel coast to be protected by a lighthouse is the SOUTH FORELAND in Kent, and this light is a warning against the dreaded Goodwin Sands. The light, which can be seen twenty-five miles away, is electric.

If coming in from the Atlantic our ship, after sighting the Bishop Rock, was making for the Bristol Channel, our next warning would be a high-power red flashing light from ROUND ISLAND, which is one of the Scillies. There are several more lights before the coast of north Devon of which the LONGSHIPS, off Land's End, is the most noticeable.

HARTLAND POINT is well worth a visit because it is built in a most spectacular position, ninety feet above the waves on a narrow isthmus of rock which is attacked by the sea on both sides. In 1925 a wall 130 feet long, twenty-eight feet wide at the base and nineteen feet high, faced with stone and backed with concrete, was built up from the shore as a protection.

Opposite Hartland is the fascinating island of LUNDY with two lights, and farther north-west, twenty-one miles from the coast of Pembrokeshire, is a group of little rocky islands called the SMALLS. For many years these dangerous rocks played havoc with shipping coming into the Bristol Channel from the north. On the largest of these islands now stands a lighthouse which flashes a light visible for eighteen miles. There is a dramatic story of heroism to be told of the Smalls lighthouse. Over one hundred years ago, before the present tower was built, only two men were in charge of the light. During a spell of bad weather one of the keepers was taken ill, and died when the time of relief was still some months ahead. What was the other man to do? He knew that his first duty was to keep the light burning, and he dare not throw the dead body of his mate into the sea, for fear that when rescue came he might be accused of murder. In his terrible plight he lashed the body upright on the gallery outside the lantern and ran up a distress signal. And when at last rescue came, the keeper who had tended the light alone, with a dead man for company, was near collapse, but he had kept the lamp burning. Ever since then remote lighthouses have been manned by three men.

56

The spectacular Gannets are very fine fishers. They are powerful, handsome sea-hawks with a wing-span of nearly six feet. Eleven of their fifteen breeding-places are round our coasts

The Great Black-Backed Gull is the largest member of the gull family.
He is not often seen in the south and west of Britain, though he is
commoner in Scotland

The Cormorant is another wonderful fisher, and he is fairly common.
The best specimens are found on the west coast of Scotland, but he can
often be seen on estuaries and tidal rivers

Another member of the gull family is
the Common Gull. In Scotland it nests
freely on grassy slopes near the coast,
and sometimes by fresh-water lochs

The Guillemot is extraordinarily affectionate and intelligent, as those well know who have rescued and cleansed a bird of oil, and kept it for a while as a pet. Here is one with its chick

A close but smaller relation to the Cormorant is the Shag. They are almost entirely birds of the wild, rocky cliffs and tiny islands off the west coast

The Razor-Bill, which is a very fast flier, is like the guillemot, but it has a great, thick, black bill. Here it is on a rocky ledge with its young

The Fulmar is an ocean bird and has a lovely, graceful, effortless flight.
You will not often see it, because it breeds in the north

There are warning lights from BARDSEY ISLAND off the Welsh coast and two very important ones called HOLYHEAD BREAK-WATER and SOUTH STACK off the island of Anglesey. Farther north still in the Irish Sea is the Isle of Man. A little rocky island to the south of it is called the Calf of Man, and south again of the Calf is the dangerous CHICKEN ROCK on which now stands one of the most magnificent lighthouses round our coasts. It is of granite and the lantern is 143 feet above the sea, but so dangerous is the reef on which it is built, and so tempestuous are the seas when the spring tides are at their highest, that waves often wash right over the light.

There are not many lighthouses on the east coast of England, because the main dangers to shipping come from sand-banks and shoals, and those are guarded by lightships about which I shall tell you something later in this chapter. But there is one very well-known lighthouse called the LONGSTONE, made famous for all time by the heroism of a lighthouse-keeper's daughter called Grace Darling.

On the evening of 6 September 1838, a steamer called the *Forfarshire* sprang a leak while passing through the narrow channel. As the water leaked into the vessel the captain decided that for safety's sake the boiler fires must be put out before the water reached them. Without her engines she soon became helpless in the storm, and although she tried to set her sails, she was eventually driven bow first on to one of the rocky islands where she broke in half. The front half of the ship remained wedged on to the rocks, but the stern portion was washed away. When morning came the lighthouse-keeper of the Longstone, whose name was William Darling, was horrified to see some survivors still clinging to the half of the wreck fixed upon the rocks. The fishermen of Bamborough also saw the wreck, but the waves were beating so fearfully against the rocks that they could not or would not launch their boats in an attempt to rescue the pitiful survivors.

From his tower William Darling could judge perhaps even better than those on shore that there was little or no chance of survival for a rowing-boat in those waters, and he too shrank from braving such dangers. But not so his daughter Grace, who tended the light with him. When she realized that the wreck could hardly hold together for more than an hour or so, she told her father that she was going to launch the lighthouse boat, and that he must come with her. At last this heroic girl had her way and, taking an oar each, the two of them somehow guided their frail craft to the wreck. God must have watched over this little boat in the dawn of that terrible morning, for, after the most frightening struggle, the nine survivors from the sixty-three souls on board were rescued. William Darling first moved five of the survivors back to the lighthouse, leaving Grace on the rock to minister to the others. He then returned on a second journey to rescue them and his brave daughter. All remained for a further two days on the lighthouse until the storm abated and they could be reached from the mainland.

Four years later, at the age of twenty-six, Grace Darling died of consumption. In the windswept chapel of St. Cuthbert on Farne Island is a slab to her memory.

The Longstone stands about two miles out to sea on a great rock in the Farne Islands off the Northumbrian coast opposite Bamborough Castle. The narrow sea-passage between the islands here and the coast has always been exceedingly dangerous in rough weather.

Other well-known lights down the east coast of England are those at Whitby, Flamborough Head, Spurn Head at the mouth of the Humber, Cromer, Lowestoft, Southwold, Orford and the North Foreland at the mouth of the Thames.

The coast of Scotland has some of the finest lighthouses in the world. Undoubtedly the most famous of them all is the wave-swept Inchcape or BELL ROCK in the busy Firth of Tay about twelve miles from the coast. The Bell Rock is a terrible place, for it is a reef two thousand feet long, lying completely submerged at high tide, right across the path of shipping.

The light on the Bell Rock is now over 150 years old, for it was in February 1811 that a twin-coloured lantern of red and white first gave its unmistakable warning to seamen coming through the North Sea approaches to the Firths of Forth and Tay. The great tower was built by Robert Stevenson, the first of the famous family of Scottish lighthouse engineers, and was even more difficult to erect than the Eddystone. The masonry, which still stands exactly as Stevenson designed and built it, is granite from the cliffs of Angus. Although this great engineer (the grandfather of Robert Louis Stevenson who wrote *Treasure Island* and *Kidnapped*) built many other lighthouses in his time, his name will always be remembered as the man who conquered the Bell Rock on which no ship has foundered for over 150 years. This is a great achievement because, in the year that Stevenson was appointed to his task, no fewer than seventy ships including a big man-of-war were lost on it.

And long, long before Stevenson raised his own worthy monument it is said that a warning bell was placed on the reef by the Abbot of Aberbrothok. The story goes that a pirate cut away this bell and you can read it for yourself in the poem called 'The Inchcape Rock' by Robert Southey.

Rocks are not the only dangers to shipping. Sand-banks and shoals are just as dangerous, and, indeed, the east coast of England has always had a terrible record of wrecks. The North Sea is shallow near our coasts, and a turmoil of conflicting tides swirls round the British Isles. The rivers running into this sea—particularly the Thames—bring silt and sand with them, and thus are the treacherous sand-banks formed. Lighthouses could not be built on sand, but light*ships* can be anchored in such dangerous places, and if you are on holiday on the east or south-east coasts, you are almost certain to see some. Usually a lightship is specially painted a striking colour such as scarlet, with the name of her station painted in enormous letters on her side.

A modern lightvessel usually has two masts with a lantern mounted amidships on a sort of trestle support about forty feet above the water-line. The light is usually electric from current generated on the ship itself. The ship, as you will see if you can look at her though a telescope or field-glass, is tubby and very strongly built.

Lightships are moored by the bow, so that they can swing round with the tide, and, as their greatest value to shipping is when the weather is at its worst, they have to be very securely anchored. The anchor is of a special type which fills with sand and sometimes weighs three tons; each ship generally has two such anchors. Unlike the lighthouse, which never moves, the lightship is never still, and the worse the weather, the more she rolls. By the most clever mechanism, however, the movement of the ship is counteracted by 'swinging' the light and reflectors on an apparatus mounted on ball-bearings, so that the lantern does not pitch and roll with the ship and the beam is kept level and steady.

Each lightship has a different sort of light, so that a sailor may never be in doubt as to where he is. Some show different-coloured beams at regular or irregular intervals; others 'flash', as do the lighthouses. When the light can no longer be seen because of fog, the crews of the lightships man the fog-horns, which blare out their warning into the gloom by means of compressed air.

Life on board a lightship is less lonely than that in a lighthouse, but far more hazardous, for the lightship is always moored in the very place which is most dangerous to shipping.

The crew of a lightvessel is usually seven—a master in charge and six seamen—who are all on board at a time. The seamen are a month afloat and then have a fortnight ashore on relief. The master is relieved every month and does turn and turn about with a second master ashore. To serve on a lightship during bad weather is very hazardous and the men sometimes suffer serious accidents as they struggle to keep the warning light burning and the ship at her moorings. Every ship now, however, has a wireless telephone so that the master is always in touch with the shore.

There are over forty lightships round our coasts now, and all are controlled by Trinity House in the same way as the lighthouses. Not all of them are visible from the shore, but many are near enough for boats to take you out in calm summer weather to look at them.

Amongst the best known are those that warn sailors of the treacherous Goodwin Sands off the coast of Kent. There are three of these lightships known as the *North*, *East* and *South Goodwin*. Shipping passes these at all hours of the day and night. A famous mark for all shipping sailing north of the Thames estuary is the *Cork* which guards the dangerous Cork ledge by Felixstowe. It is fairly close to the shore off the Essex–Suffolk coasts. There are several treacherous sand-banks hereabouts guarded by *Galloper*, the *Kentish Knock* and the *Long-Sand*. The Girdler Sands are also protected by three more lightships, while farther north off the Norfolk coast the notorious Haisborough Sands, which have accounted for many wrecks, are marked by the *Haisborough* lightvessel and a lighthouse on the shore, too.

Another world-famous lightship which you are not so likely to see is the *Seven Stones*, moored between the Scilly Islands and Land's End. This ship marks a group of rocks that show seven cruel fangs when the tide goes down. This position must surely be the most exposed of any round our coasts for a lightship. Sailors refer to this place and the light merely as 'The Stones'.

I have only room to tell you about a few of these specially constructed vessels and their brave crews, but they are all as vital to the safety of the shipping of all nations as the lighthouses.

From their stations and posts usually on cliff-tops Her Majesty's Coast-Guards keep watch over the six thousand miles of coastline of Great Britain and Northern Ireland. One day when you are on holiday you may see a coast-guard look-out hut. In fine weather, when the sea is calm, the hut may be empty, for in some places round the coast watch is only kept in bad weather and then, of course, by day and night. In other places where the sea or coast is specially dangerous a look-out or watcher is always on duty.

You will recognize coast-guards by their navy-blue uniform and the flash 'H.M. Coast-Guard' on their shoulders, but they are helped by a part-time voluntary service called the Coast Life-Saving Corps. These men and women who give up much of their spare time to help the coast-guards do all sorts of jobs. Some keep watch from the look-out huts; some take telephone messages; some act as special messengers and others belong to the Life-Saving Companies which are ready to be called out day and night to rescue the crew of a stranded or wrecked ship. There are over 6,500 of these volunteers.

The coast-guard's duty and privilege is the saving of life, and there can be no work in the world more worth while than this. Just over one hundred years ago, when the service was founded, its main job was the prevention of smuggling, and then, I've no doubt, the coast-guard did more fighting than life-saving! In ordinary weather today he does little more than watch to see if shipping or aircraft over the sea are in danger. He can, of course, take signals from passing ships and with his radio telephone speak to the nearest lighthouse or lightship. But, in the summer holiday months, he is kept busy rescuing boys and girls, and grown-ups too, who ought to have more sense than to get themselves cut off by the tide or trapped on cliffs, or who lose control of a rubber dinghy or rowing-boat in which they ventured out alone. I warned you in my first chapter about these dangers, but the coast-guards are always ready to help. They have special ladders for cliff rescues and wear head-guards like wicker baskets to protect their heads from falling rocks and stones.

But it is in bad weather that he is most needed. On the days when you and I prefer to shelter indoors and sit round the fire as the gale roars round the chimney-pots, and on the nights when rain lashes the bedroom window, that is when the coast-guard looks to see if his life-saving equipment is in order and warns his mates that they may soon be wanted.

Let us see what happens in the look-out hut on the top of the cliff on such an evening. The rain is beating against the windows, so that sea and sky are one watery, grey blur. The coast-guard on duty—there are probably four men permanently at this station—has already been warned by telephone from the next station down the coast that a tramp steamer, apparently in some difficulty, is beating up against wind and getting dangerously near the shore. Our coast-guard watches the darkening waste of sea and sky carefully. He knows where to look. He knows every inch of the coast, where the dangerous currents run and where they will carry a ship out of control.

The dusk deepens, and then, just where he expected, he sees a speck against the grey background of the sea and knows it is a ship. As he reaches for the telephone, a thin line of fire streaks up into the sky and bursts like a scarlet flower opening in the sun.

The rocket distress signal!

The coast-guard never puts to sea for rescue work, and acts only when the ship runs aground or strikes a rock. It is the life-boat, as you know, which puts to sea, and the coast-guard acts as an 'intelligence service' to the life-boat. Our coast-guard is confident that the ship has fired her distress signal because she struck some rocks about five hundred yards from the shore, and although he is certain that the life-boat crew, six miles down the coast, will have seen the rocket, his first duty is to telephone a warning to them. He gives them the precise position of the wreck and tells them that the coast-guards are going into action at once.

Even while he is speaking, another rocket rises into the gloom, and he knows that there is no more time to waste. As he puts down the receiver he hears a heavy boom—the other coast-guards on the station are firing a maroon as a signal to the trained men of the Coast Life-Saving Corps. A maroon is a firework which explodes with a very loud noise, and as the storm has increased, the men concerned in the near-by village have almost certainly been listening for it.

The next job is to take the life-saving apparatus, which is kept ready in a trailer to be towed by a near-by lorry, to the part of the coast nearest to the doomed ship.

Try to imagine that you are taking part in the rescue.

It is dark now. The wind is roaring over the top of the cliff, and down below the great waves are thundering on the beach. Spray and rain beat into our faces as we run down the rough road from the station towards the shed where the apparatus is kept. The first men of the Life-Saving Corps are flinging back the doors of the shed as we arrive. A big lorry, with the engine throbbing, has been backed in as close as possible, while the rest of the crew pull out the loaded trailer and fix it to the back, and then we all climb aboard and roar and clatter out into the night. Down the road we lurch and turn into the main road for a mile, then down another lane which leads us to the beach, and almost before we can jump out the crew is unloading the lorry. The first job now is to make communication with the ship, which can only be seen by the lights she is showing. The life-saving crew does this by firing a rocket, to which is attached a length of light rope, *over* the wreck, so that the rope falls across the deck. It is easier to rescue men by this means from the shore than from the top of a cliff. We had better stand back out of the way. You will see that the rocket machine stands at an angle on two legs, and that the rocket itself, which must carry seven hundred yards of one-inch rope, is over two feet long. It is about sixteen pounds in weight, so you will not be surprised when it goes off towards the wreck with a roar and a tail of fire, aimed like a bullet from a gun. As you know, all rockets must be fixed to a stick, and this stick is nine feet six inches long, and the rope is passed through a hole at its end.

We can watch the fiery tail of the rocket streak up into the night and then fall into the blackness beyond the wreck. One of the life-saving crew turns and shouts through the wind that the rocket has flown straight and true and that the line has reached the ship. A signal, winking from the wreck, confirms this.

It is difficult in the confusion and darkness to see exactly what is happening, but now that the life-line has reached the ship, there is every chance that the crew can be brought safely to land, and that the life-boat that is even now on her way will not be needed.

The crew on the wreck now pull in the life-line, to which is attached what is called the 'whip'. The whip is an endless length of rope running through an ordinary pulley block, so that when one loop is made fast, say, to the mast of the ship, and the other is firmly attached at our end, the heavy three-inch hawser can be hauled across. Fixed to the hawser is a board with a message of instruction printed in several languages. Once this heavy rope is made fast to the mast, our crew can send over the breeches-buoy by the whip. In fine weather you would enjoy a ride in the breeches-buoy, for it is only a cork life-belt fitted with 'breeches' of brown canvas, through which you can put your legs. It is slung by four ropes from a block which runs on the thick hawser and is, of course, hauled by the endless rope of the whip.

By now, I daresay, the life-boat has arrived, but the first member of the crew from the wreck is now coming across in the breeches-buoy. He is a white-faced lad of about sixteen, who wipes the water out of his eyes, splutters, and then grins his thanks as he is helped out on to the shingle.

Back again goes the buoy. Again the light flashes from the wreck, and again our life-savers haul back another man from certain death. The storm rages on and the waves thunder on the beach and fill the air with spray, which tastes salt on our lips. The life-boat flashes signals, and we reply as the last man—the captain —is hauled across. He looks grim and tired, and as he is helped out we notice that he is carrying a big metal box—the ship's papers. He tells the life-saving crew that the ship cannot last many more minutes.

This is how the coast-guard works. He is trained to save life, and his greatest work is always done when the weather is at its worst. So when you are next at the seaside and watch the ships go by, give a thought to the men in the lighthouses and the lightships and to the coast-guards, and if you get a chance, watch them at their work.

A beautiful flowering shrub often seen in seaside gardens is the Fuchsia, with its solitary
hanging flowers of rich red and purple,
blooming from June on into the autumn

Eddystone Lighthouse, Devon

The most attractive and typical of all our seaside flowers is the Thrift, which looks its best growing in masses on the edge of cliffs. It thrives equally well near the shore on sand dunes

Start Point Lighthouse, Devon

Berry Head Lighthouse, Devon

Trevose Lighthouse, Cornwall

Sevenstones Lightship off
the Cornish coast

When Sea-Lavender is growing thickly, it is a splendid sight and easy to identify. It is no relation of the fragrant lavender in our gardens

Two of Her Majesty's Coast-Guard stations at (*above*) the Lizard, and (*below*) Cape Cornwall

Sea-Aster

Sea-Campion

7

Around Our Coasts

I'm sure you'll enjoy this chapter more with a map of Britain. I hope you like maps as much as I do because, when I was working on this book and looking at an atlas, I was reminded of a poem I once read about a map. I found it at last and print it here for you. I like it because it describes our islands as 'the butt of many seas that shaped its landscape . . .'.

How tiny England is this map will show,
*   And how she is the butt of many seas*
*   That shaped its landscape to its subtleties,*
How few her rivers are, her hills how low.
This map will tell you faintly of her towns
*   (Pin-point for London, Thames a thread of hair),*
But will not tell of dewponds on the Downs,
*   Or how the leaves of Warwick green the air.*
This map will tell you nothing of the way
*   The coltish April skips across her skies,*
*   Nor how, in Autumn nights, the curlew cries,*
Or thrush or blackbird harmonise in May.
*   For these such things consult that wiser chart*
*   Engraved upon the exiled English heart.*

James Walker

THIS CHAPTER IS a special sort of journey. When I first planned this book, I was sure that I should have to tell you something of what you would see if you took an imaginary trip by sea—or even by helicopter—round the coasts of Britain. But the more I thought about this and the longer I looked at maps, the more certain I became that I should have to write another book to do it properly. One chapter could never be enough, and even when I tried to write it I thought it was like a geography lesson and was sure you wouldn't want that. So what was I to do? Read on now and I hope you will like the answer, because I decided that the only way was to tell you about some of the places which I have actually explored myself and where I have had happy holidays.

Before we start you will remember that our land was once joined to the mainland of Europe, but the narrow, twenty-mile Channel, which up till now has separated us from France, has saved us from invasion by sea since the day when William the Conqueror landed in Pevensey Bay on the Sussex coast in 1066. Today, when it is possible to fly to Europe in a few minutes, we can no longer 'keep ourselves to ourselves' as once we did, even if we wanted to do so, and in your lifetime it may be that the Channel Tunnel from Dover to the French coast will be built.

Nevertheless, I'm sure that because we live on an island we've always been a nation of sailors and adventurers and have gone down to the sea in ships through all our history, and I think that the sea will always mean a great deal to a Briton.

The British Isles, although so small, boast the most varied and romantic coastline of any islands in the world, and almost every mile of it would be suitable for some sort of holiday. There is something for everybody—big resorts with piers and bands and gleaming promenades, great ports with ships waiting in the docks, little fishing villages, ugly bungalow towns, and cliffs and sands and beaches of many kinds and colours.

Let's begin our journey together on the south coast which I know so well because I was born in Sussex and live there now. Imagine that we board our vessel at Dover below the great white cliffs which are so often the first glimpse of England seen by the traveller coming home. Not many people travelling to Europe from England have time to explore the crowded little town, because they only step from the train into the cross-channel steamer. Much of our history has been made here and there's a great castle frowning on the top of the cliffs. Dover is not attractive but remember that it is probably the oldest gateway to England.

In the last war it was shelled and bombed by the enemy and most of the population slept at night in deep caves in the cliffs. It is one of the seven Cinque Ports, which in the Middle Ages were responsible for the sea defence of our country. The other ports are Hastings, Winchelsea, Rye, New Romney, Hythe and Sandwich, and the British Navy developed from the ships which were built in these ports from oak grown in the forests of the Sussex Weald.

As we sail west, we pass Folkestone from which the Channel steamers sail to Boulogne. This is a big seaside resort built mainly on the top of the cliffs. Next Hythe, now a sleepy little town just inland, and if you ever go there you will find it specially interesting for two reasons. Firstly it is the end of the Royal Military Canal which was built to make things difficult for Napoleon, if his armies ever landed on the flat coast hereabouts. You can take a rowing-boat out on this canal, remembering that, although often expected, no invading armies have ever landed here. Hythe is also the terminus of the most exciting and efficient miniature railway in Britain—the Hythe, Romney and Dymchurch Light Railway—which runs a regular service of passenger trains pulled by wonderful small-scale model steam locomotives from Hythe to Dungeness. I've been many times on these splendid little trains and so should you when you get the chance.

Look at your map now and you will see that the country inland between Hythe and Rye is called Romney Marsh—a strange green and white land given over to the rearing of a famous breed of sheep which have been sent out to many parts of the world. Most of the eastern side of the Marsh was drained and reclaimed in Norman times, though the Romans probably built the first town from which it gets its name—Romney. This little triangle of lovely country has a long and exciting association with smuggling. Your map shows you how near it is to the coast of France, and it is true that at one time the Marsh people prospered by shipping as much wool out of the country as brandy and lace were brought in from France. Once there was a time when an honest man had no chance of making a livelihood on the Marsh, for squire and parson and farmer were all engaged in smuggling. Many are the tales told of mysterious riders whose faces glowed with an evil green light as they galloped the Marsh at night, until every door was barred and every window shuttered as 'the gentlemen rode by'. Many were the battles between the King's men and the 'Owlers' as those who smuggled out wool were called.

Sailing west we next round the great desert of shingle known as Dungeness. You can't mistake it because of the new lighthouse, mentioned in Chapter 6. A new nuclear power station to supply electricity to the south of England is also being built here. This strange place is well known to bird lovers because many of those birds which come to us in the spring from the sunnier south cross the coast just here and sometimes rest in the lonely wastes.

Each year Dungeness pushes itself out a little farther into the Channel because the headland grows as the tides pile up the pebbles. The shingle drops sheer into deep water here so that quite large ships can anchor close in and shelter in a storm behind the Ness.

After rounding this headland we are in Rye Bay and can see the little town of Rye, a huddle of red roofs on its pyramid of rock which is now about two miles from the sea, although once the waves of the Channel washed its walls.

As we sail across Rye Bay, we can see behind Rye and the Marsh the long line of higher ground which shows where the sea used to reach and it's not difficult to imagine the waves beating against these inland cliffs. About two miles to the west of Rye all that is left of her sister Cinque Port, Winchelsea, drowses on a wooded hill. The approaches to Winchelsea are still guarded by three ruined gateways. Winchelsea Beach, now protected by a sturdy sea wall, was where I spent my first seaside holiday in a coast-guard's cottage. Here I first felt the magic of the road that leads to the sea, and here I first saw sea-poppies blowing in the shingle and sea-lavender purple on the edge of the sheep-dotted marsh. Here I watched the warning light of Dungeness as darkness fell and the answering wink of the lighthouse at Griz Nez on the French coast. Winchelsea Beach is very different now but the air is still as sweet and the waves still pound up the shingle when the tide is high, and the gulls still sail effortlessly in the south-west wind.

Next we see the high sandstone cliffs, called the Fire Hills because they are so often ablaze with golden gorse, at Fairlight, and then Hastings and St. Leonard's as we sail along the Sussex coast. Eastbourne is where the South Downs run into the sea at Beachy Head, but before we get there, there is more low-lying marshland known as Pevensey Levels. There are the ruins of an enormous castle at Pevensey. After Eastbourne, which is hidden behind the great chalk cliffs, we soon come to Newhaven from where the Channel steamers sail to Dieppe and where the Sussex Ouse runs out to the sea. Smugglers used this river, too, not so very many years ago. The cliffs on this stretch of coast are all of chalk, and you will notice a row of headlands called the Seven Sisters which you can count for yourself. You can't miss Brighton and Hove and their spectacular sea-fronts and the Downs behind, and it is about here that I might want to land for a while for I am only twelve miles from home. You will see a great power station right on the coast between Hove and Shoreham which has a harbour almost at the muddy mouth of the River Adur. On the Downs behind is the superb chapel of Lancing College which is a landmark to all sailors.

Now the coast is dull and although I've been to such seaside resorts as Bognor Regis and Littlehampton, I don't know much about them. Neither can I tell you more than you probably know about Portsmouth, Southampton and Bournemouth. But the Isle of Wight, sometimes and rightly called the Garden Isle, is a very different matter, for although so close to the mainland it is like another miniature country. The waters round the Wight are a yachtsman's paradise and all the cliffs and beaches are wonderful. The channel between the north coast of the island, and the mainland and Southampton Water and the entrance to Southampton Water, where the great liners go, is called the Solent, while that between Portsmouth and the Island is Spithead. There are two important lighthouses to warn ships of the dangerous coasts— St. Catherine's in the south and the Needles to the west. I know a beach at Alum Bay where the cliffs of sandstone are streaked with rainbow colours and it is possible to fill a glass bottle with layers of different-coloured sands. The steep wooded valleys running down to the sea in the Isle of Wight are called chines.

After the coast of Hampshire we shall see the hills and cliffs of Dorset, and the part of this beautiful country I know best is the little town of Lyme Regis with its gently curving stone wall, which is called the Cobb, protecting its tiny harbour. I got to know it because a schoolgirl I had never met wrote to me once from Lyme and asked me to write a story about the town in which she lived, because she thought it would make an exciting and romantic background. And so it did.

Lyme has been used by smugglers and a battle of the Civil War was fought there. Between it and the little Devon town of Seaton is an unusual stretch of wild country where there was a landslip over a hundred years ago. Then part of the cliffs slid down towards the sea and settled at a lower level, so making a mysterious 'secret kingdom' ready for you to explore one day.

Drake and Ralegh and many other British seamen-adventurers sailed out from Devon, and her red cliffs are famed throughout the world. This beautiful county has two sea-boards—one to the north and one to the south. I must remind you of Plymouth in the south, but I have only been there when I was staying on Dartmoor. Those who live in Devon claim that Plymouth harbour is the finest and most beautiful in Britain and so I think it is. From here Sir Francis Drake sailed out with his tiny navy to beat the Spanish Armada, for Plymouth was the chief naval base of the first Queen Elizabeth. It seems fitting that the little wooded island you will see at the entrance to the harbour should be called Drake's Island.

I wish I knew Cornwall better for both the north and south coasts are magnificent. I hope you will go there many times and discover much that I have missed. For centuries the granite cliffs have been pounded by the rollers of the Atlantic and here are exciting little coves, beaches of gleaming sand and caves used by smugglers. Listen to the names of some of the little towns on this romantic southern coast of the Duchy of Cornwall—Looe, Polperro, Mevagissey, St. Anthony-in-Roseland, Coverack, Marazion, Mullion, Mousehole and Lamorna Cove. If you've ever been to this coast and stood in the dusk on one of the beaches of these coves, it's not difficult to imagine a scene as the sun goes down. Here, waiting where you now stand, there would be perhaps six rough, bearded men each with a hardy little pony. These men would be very poorly dressed for, in the eighteenth century, there was severe poverty in Cornwall, and indeed there was little that many of the men with families could do besides smuggling. Anyway, here they would sit in the darkness until the keen eyes of one of them would see a small boat struggling through the breakers. They would help to haul it in and quickly unload the kegs of brandy, the packets of lace and tobacco or barrels of rum, and load these on the backs of the ponies. A few muttered words and the boat would be pushed off, and then the men would hurry the laden ponies up the rocky paths to the inland villages where the goods were eagerly awaited. There must have been many a fight in those days between the smugglers and the soldiers or revenue men.

Huddled on the coast to the north of Mount's Bay is the little town of Marazion and opposite, out at sea, is St. Michael's Mount

with its castle-crowned height and wooded slopes. A stone cause-
way crosses the smooth sands between Marazion and the Mount,
but you can only cross to the island by foot at low tide. And you
must be very careful, too, because the tide rushes across the sand
dangerously fast and it is easy to be cut off. I'm sure you will be as
thrilled by this exciting place as I was when I first went there.
I've been to Land's End, too, and if you go, remember that these
granite cliffs are the westernmost tip of Britain. The headland
runs one and a half miles out to sea and the force of the Atlantic
waves here is so strong that the towering, weather-worn granite
cliffs are being gradually worn away.

You'll be enchanted by the north coast of Cornwall for it is
romantic country. Perhaps there is no place in England so rich in
history and legend as Tintagel, away to the north of Newquay
near Boscastle. This really is one of the most spectacular places I
have ever seen, for the massive ruin of the castle stands on a great
hill joined to the mainland by a narrow tongue of rock. Here,
tradition says, was chivalry born, for Tintagel was the home of
King Arthur and his Knights of the Round Table. It is true that
you can enter the ruin through the remains of a stone doorway,
but the facts seem to be that the castle itself is a twelfth-century
fortress and therefore King Arthur could not possibly have lived
in it. All the same, as you pass through that ancient doorway it
won't be difficult for you to imagine that you are exploring a
courtyard that Sir Galahad or the wizard Merlin may have
trodden. Even if this is all myth you'll agree, I'm sure, that
Tintagel is exactly the sort of romantic place which should have
been used by King Arthur and the flower of chivalry.

The coast of north Devon begins near Hartland Point, and the
places I know near here are Barnstaple, Bideford and a little
village of white cottages called Appledore, where the rivers Taw
and Torridge race out to sea. As you sail up the Bristol Channel
past Lynton and Lynmouth you will see the heights of Exmoor
inland.

The next place I can tell you about is on the opposite side of the
Channel on the western side of Carmarthen Bay in Wales. This
is a wonderful coast with cliffs and golden sands, and the little
town I know best is Tenby with its colour-washed houses standing
high on the cliffs above two bays. South of Tenby is Caldy Island
which has a monastery into which no women are allowed. Last
time I was at Tenby I tried for three days to get over to Caldy,
but the sea was too rough and none of the fishermen would risk

the crossing. If you like islands as much as I do, you will want to explore Caldy where the thrift blows on the cliff-tops and the sea-birds cry.

I wish I knew the rest of Wales better, but I can only tell you that the coastline of Cardigan Bay offers wonderful stretches of sand and such seaside towns as Aberystwyth, Aberdovey and Barmouth. A few miles up the estuary from the latter is Dol-gelley where I once stayed before climbing Cader Idris, which is not as difficult as it sounds although it is nearly 3,000 feet high.

Farther north still in Caernarvon Bay are the islands of Anglesey and Holyhead. Look at the map again and you will see that ancient Caernarvon itself is on the mainland side of the Menai Straits. Wales is famous for its castles and that at Caernarvon is more famous than most, for it is the largest and best preserved in Britain and the second biggest in Europe. I'm trying hard not to make this chapter like a lesson, but when I explore a place I want to know things like this. History becomes real and alive at places like Caernarvon when you can walk where King Edward I must have watched his builders begin work on his great castle in 1284. Here, by ancient tradition, each Prince of Wales is presented to the people.

I hope you'll be able to explore Anglesey and Holyhead. The Irish mail-trains from Euston are carried across the Menai Straits by an unusual tubular bridge built by the famous Robert Stephen-son over a hundred years ago and close by is the road suspension-bridge. When you cross it in a car remember that this is the bridge which carried the old mail-coaches to Holyhead as long ago as 1826. I liked Holyhead because I like trains and boats. It's been the port for Ireland for hundreds of years and the long trains run right up to the landing quay. Holyhead mountain, which really marks the entrance to the Irish Sea is, we are told by geologists, made of the oldest known rock in the world. There are 365 steps leading down the face of the precipice. I was not able to stay long in Anglesey and Holyhead, but I'm sure you could have a grand holiday on the wonderful beaches of these islands.

On all our family holidays we have always kept a diary in which everybody takes a daily turn to write a description of what we have done and seen, and in which we stick our snaps later.

I am always wanting to go back to Scotland, and wonder why so many people go abroad for their holidays when Scotland is on our doorstep. Look again at your map at the magnificent western coast of this beautiful country. You will see that it is broken up by many islands the names of which spell magic to Scots in all parts of the world. As I re-read the diary of our last visit to Connell Ferry near Oban (which is a splendid centre for exploring) many wonderful memories come crowding back. If you are able to view this superb coastline from the sea and sail up into the Atlantic from the Irish Sea, you will see the Isle of Arran to the north and then the islands of Islay and Jura.

In the Firth of Lorne opposite the island of Mull is Oban, and the country behind it is superb. Here are the Western Highlands with sinister Glencoe, Fort William and the chain of lochs, called the Caledonian Canal, not far away. But it is the Western Isles, stretching in a great arc, 130 miles long and forty miles off the coast, that really call. These islands, facing the full force of the Atlantic breakers, consist of about one hundred inhabited islets, every loch and creek of which was probably seen by the pillaging Vikings. On every headland and shore these fierce marauders were welcomed with the ring of steel by those ancestors of Highlanders with the same names whom you may meet and speak with today.

You must explore these islands for yourself. From Oban, steamers will take you round the Isle of Mull and then to the snowy white beaches of Iona, the small island with the graves of two score of Scottish, Irish and Norwegian kings, and an austere cathedral now most wonderfully restored. You should then see the tiny, curiously shaped isle of Staffa. Twice we tried to visit Staffa but each time the sea was too rough to risk a landing and the island was smothered in spray. Staffa is remarkable because its bleak cliffs consist of great columns of an unusual type of black rock called basalt. These cliffs are pierced by many caverns, the best known of which is Fingal's Cave. The booming of the waves in these caves produces a weird sound like the deep notes of a mighty organ.

The chief town in Mull is Tobermory. It is believed that in the harbour one of the ships of the Spanish Armada was sunk with gold still in its holds. Attempts with divers are, I believe, still being made to find this treasure, and when I was at Tobermory I saw the salvage vessel which they were using in the harbour.

I wish I could tell you more from personal knowledge about Scotland, but I shall go back there again and explore the rugged and romantic Western Isles as soon as I can.

The next part of our coastline I would like to introduce you to is that of Yorkshire by Whitby. This is one of my favourite seaside towns and I've written two adventure stories set in its narrow streets and in the dramatic country behind it. Yorkshire, like Scotland, tempts me constantly to return and I doubt if you will be able to resist its spell either.

Whitby is built on two hills—one on each side of the mouth of the river Esk which forms a harbour for a fishing fleet. On one hill is the ruined abbey of St. Hilda and an unusual-looking church with its graveyard on the very edge of the cliff. There's a fish-market at Whitby and it's a grand sight to see the trawlers racing into the harbour with their holds full of fish. There are two places called Staithes and Robin Hood's Bay close by and both have great character. They were fishing villages once, but I think there were more artists than fishermen about when I was last there. I do not know why Robin Hood's Bay was so called but now it is generally referred to as Bay by those who live there on each side of a narrow street almost too steep for cars. I'm sure that smugglers must have used both these places in the past, and indeed there is a track running from Bay to the high road between Pickering and Whitby at a hamlet called Saltersgate. The latter is well-named, for this ancient way was once a salt road and later was used by fish-pedlars. I've walked this track and had tea in the Saltersgate Inn.

The country directly behind Robin Hood's Bay is the desolate Fylingdales Moor which for many years has been used by the Army but on which is now being built a great detector of guided missiles. It's strange to remember that only a few miles away you can walk on the actual stones of a road made by the Romans for their invading armies over two thousand years ago. It can be reached easily from Goathland.

I know more about the inland country of Yorkshire than the coast, but I have been to Scarborough and watched cricket there in September and you will like this delightful town, too. It stands between two bays, and on the headland between them are the ruins of a castle which was one of the strongholds of the north and was built in King Stephen's reign.

I'm looking at the map again and realizing how lucky I have been to have seen so much of our exciting coastline, and the next stretch I want to tell you about is the great bulge of Norfolk. Some of my happiest holidays have been spent at little places on the north coast of this county that you would hardly notice from the sea. They are all worth exploring if you travel on the coast road between Hunstanton with its enormous stretch of sands and

Cromer standing proudly on its crumbling cliffs. This is flat country but of great beauty. The skies are wide and the cloud effects unforgettable and somehow scarlet poppies always seem to be blooming in summer in the big corn-fields.

Not far from Wells-next-the-Sea is a sandy island called Scolt Head which is a wonderful bird sanctuary. Then there is Blakeney at the head of a creek much used by sailing enthusiasts. There's a very fine church here with a narrow, chimney-like tower beside the big belfry at the west end. This smaller tower was specially built so that a beacon fire could be lit at the top as a warning to sailors battling down the coast in a north-easterly gale. This is one of the most dangerous parts of our coasts because, although there are no rocks, there are many treacherous sand-banks out at sea. Virtually all the cliffs from here to the mouth of the Thames are soft and sandy, and the hungry North Sea is gradually eating the coast away.

Lower down this sandy coast are the towns of Great Yarmouth and Lowestoft—both are seaside resorts and ports used by the herring fleets. Inland here are the famous Norfolk Broads.

Lowestoft is in Suffolk and its southern suburb of Pakefield is in grave danger from the sea; a little farther south is the delightful little town of Southwold with its white lighthouse rising above the roof-tops. Then come the remains of Dunwich, once the greatest port of East Anglia. You'll see nothing but the line of sandy cliffs from the sea, for the few houses left are now inland, but at very low tide can sometimes be found, not only treasures left by those who lived in Dunwich hundreds of years ago, but the bones of those who were buried round the six churches of the ancient port. It is said that sometimes, if you listen carefully, you can hear the sound of drowned church bells, but I have never done so!

Behind the coast at Orford Ness, a few miles south of Alde-burgh, is the extraordinary river Ore, which runs just inland up beyond Orford to become the river Alde. Your map—if it is big enough—will show you this remarkable stretch of water, but it's more fun to go one day and see it for yourself.

Now I have not much more to tell you on our imaginary voyage, for we are nearly at the mouth of the Thames.

Many years ago I had a holiday at Felixstowe where the pier is very long indeed, and of course I've been to Harwich at the mouth of the rivers Stour and Orwell. From this port ships sail to Antwerp and the Hook of Holland.

Even if you only visited the places to which I have been in my lifetime you would have seen a coastline of infinite variety. You will have looked up at cliffs of chalk, of sandstone and of granite. You will have seen green pastures running down to the sea, stretches of gleaming sand and beaches of smooth shingle. You will have heard the roar of the Atlantic surf pounding our western seaboard, and the hungry North Sea slyly eating away the soft cliffs of East Anglia.

You will have seen romantic islands, muddy estuaries, the ruins of great castles and the spires and belfries of churches, and on your voyage, even if you didn't stop, you will have seen those parts of our coast where our history has been made.

Where else in the whole world could you see so much of interest and of beauty in so short a time?

8

The Road to the Sea

At the beginning of this book I told you something about the thrill of a road that leads to the sea, and now that we are nearing the end I want to take you on an imaginary journey down such a road. I'm sure you will soon catch something of its magic.

Sooner or later we shall come to a turn in our road and see before us the horizon—that sharp line dividing sea and sky—which is a promise of the delights of smooth sand and rock-pools and much else besides. The flowers are different, many of the trees are a different shape from those growing inland, the sea-birds wheel and cry overhead and on the wind comes the sound of the everlasting waves.

I'M SURE THAT the first thing we shall notice as our road approaches the sea-shore is the strength and savour of the wind. There always seems to be a breeze blowing off the sea, and it comes with that exciting, never-to-be-forgotten smell of salt and seaweed that is like no other smell in the world.

It is this wind, nearly always blowing from the same quarter— in Britain, what is called the prevailing wind comes from the south-west—which shapes those trees growing near the shore. As we walk down our lane you will see that the trees are shorter and sturdier than those growing farther inland and that their branches almost all lean in the same direction away from the sea. I know a wood of ash trees in a fold of the South Downs, where every tree is stunted, and the branches, forced when they were young and pliant by the south-westerly gales, have had no chance to grow where they will.

The most common trees by the sea-shore seem to be the HAWTHORN and the PINE which are both hardy and strong. The hawthorn is sometimes called the MAY tree and you'll know it because the gnarled and twisted trunks suggest that the trees are very old. The branches grow thickly and the lovely flowers of white or pink, which appear at the end of April and beginning of May, are heavily scented and protected by sharp spikes. No doubt you know that in late autumn the hawthorn is usually covered with a mass of clustered, scarlet berries called haws, and birds are very fond of these. Strong as are these splendid trees, their shape is changed by the wind when they are young.

Everyone knows the pine tree and the cones which it drops ready for us to collect and use as fire lighters. The SCOTS PINE is the commonest of these trees and may grow to a height of a hundred feet. The bark is pinky brown in colour and sometimes the lower branches die and fall. You'll notice that pitch and resin ooze from the trunk. Pines prefer sandy soil, but they don't seem to mind the salt in the air and are strong enough to stand up to most gales. We shall almost certainly see some pines near our road to the sea.

Perhaps we shall soon come to a cottage and here, in the front garden or against the wall, we may be lucky and see a TAMARISK which is probably the most unusual of the trees found only by the sea. It prefers a kindly climate and you will see lots of them on our south-west coasts such as in Devon and Cornwall, and there are some in Sussex too. In a garden it does not grow much larger than a bush and it's rarely more than twenty feet high even when flourishing on sand dunes, but it is easy to recognize because its leaves are tiny and feathery and of a beautiful bluish green. It looks its best between July and September when the rose-pink flowers are blooming. These are tiny and are massed into long spikes growing so closely together that they look like plumes.

Somebody once told me that the tamarisk was first brought to Britain by smugglers over three hundred years ago. It certainly flourishes in France and Spain and we're lucky to have it here. I've seen it planted successfully as a hedge in a seaside garden, and it thrives in a sandy soil and stands up well against gales and salt spray.

Another beautiful flowering shrub often seen in seaside gardens, although it is also cultivated elsewhere, is the FUCHSIA with its solitary hanging flowers of rich red and purple. I think of them as miniature Chinese lanterns and you will see them blooming from June on into the autumn. I remember a long fuchsia hedge in Cornwall and I've seen them flowering on the west coast of Scotland too.

Another shrub we may see planted to act as a wind-break is SEA-BUCKTHORN. This attractive bush is sometimes ten feet high. Along the east coast of Britain it grows quite thickly on sand dunes but I have also seen it in a Sussex garden. The bark is grey and some of the twigs are sharply spiked, while the narrow leaves are greenish grey, but it is not until autumn that the sea-buck-thorn looks its best, for then the bush is covered with yellow berries rather like tiny oranges.

As we get nearer to the sea we shall notice that such common flowers and weeds as thistles and dandelions are sturdier and shorter in their growth than they are in a country lane. Look carefully and you will see that their leaves are much thicker and 'fleshier' than usual, and this is because these plants must store more water in their leaves as they don't like the salt in the air and soil by the seaside.

Now perhaps our road rises a little to the crest of the sand-hills, with the sea directly below us, and if we explore either to left or right we shall see many strange flowers and plants. There are lots of different kinds of grasses, but there is one in particular, called SAND-SEDGE or SEA-SEDGE, which helps to keep the sand-hills from breaking up. Although it only grows to a height of a few inches, its roots are very strong.

Another grass which serves the same purpose is MARRAM

GRASS, which grows in clumps and binds the sand together with its roots. Be careful how you handle marram, however, because the leaves are sharp and can cut your fingers badly. Once this grass was much used for thatching the roofs of seaside cottages, because it is so tough.

Another attractive plant which grows on the sand-hills or in the loose sand between the dunes is the SEA-BINDWEED or CON-VOLVULUS. This plant is, of course, a close relation to the bind-weed which is such a nuisance in many gardens. The seaside variety does not climb nor twine and never grows more than about six inches high. The stems which it sends out cling close to the sand and its long, spreading roots help, like those of the marram grass, to bind the sand of the dunes. The leaves are smooth, thick and shiny and the flowers, which are surprisingly large for the size of the plant—about one and a half inches across, bloom between June and August. They are pink with yellowish or red streaks on them and are borne singly on stalks about six inches high. They are very handsome.

You may see the sea-bindweed sometimes in shingle, but it prefers sand and is found generally all round our coasts, although it is rarer on the east coast.

I think the most attractive and typical of all our seaside flowers is the THRIFT or SEA-PINK. It is quite common and easy to recognize because it is like the thrift which is grown in parks and rock-gardens. It looks its best growing in masses on the edge of cliffs and even in crevices on the cliff itself, but it thrives equally well near the shore, on sand dunes, and even on walls close to the sea. The leaves are low and grass-like and the comparatively tall stalks (up to twelve inches high) carry a tight, round head of delightful pink blossom from April until September. I've also heard this flower called the sea-gilliflower, but whatever its name it flourishes where the salt winds blow.

Thrift belongs to the same plant family as SEA-LAVENDER which blooms in July and August, but is no relation to the fragrant lavender in our gardens. There are several different kinds of sea-lavender, the most common variety of which usually grows in salt marshes in England and Wales. The best I ever saw was in August on a marsh in Norfolk. The plant sends up flowering shoots about six inches high and the lilac-coloured blooms are on stems without leaves. When sea-lavender is growing thickly it is a splendid sight and is easy to identify. Another close relation which you can find growing on cliffs and on rocks by the sea is ROCK SEA-LAVENDER.

The Spurge Hawk-Moth is rare and
flies very quickly. Its small wings have
a most beautiful rose tint

Launching the Fleetwood life-boat

Hawthorn shaped by the sea-wind

The Thrift Clearwing, which is fairly
common, hovers rather like a fly over
the clumps of pink thrift

Tamarisk

Sea-Buckthorn

Samphire

Sea-Bindweed

Yellow-Horned Poppy

Spectacular and unmistakable is the handsome Peacock butterfly, on the wing in August and September. On each of its velvety, brownish red wings is the bold badge of a 'peacock's eye'

Sea-Holly

Sea-Spurge

The Red Admiral can sometimes be seen
coming in over the waves and up the road
to the sea

The flowers of this plant are a deeper colour than the common variety and the stems shorter and more branched, and it seems to prefer the west coast.

There are several unusual flowers and things to see on a salt marsh, which is usually on very low ground at the estuary of a river or behind sand dunes or a shingle bank which keeps back the sea. The most exciting marsh that I have ever found is behind such a bank between the villages of Walberswick and Dunwich on the Suffolk coast just south of the attractive little town of Southwold. This marsh is criss-crossed with deep dykes fringed with bullrushes, and you could easily lose your way and be drowned if you tried to walk across in the dark or in a fog. A track along the land side, beneath the great bank beyond which the sea roars up the beach, is just wide enough for two to walk abreast. As you walk you will have to be careful not to tread on the beautiful SEA-ASTERS with their big purple flowers with golden centres. This plant is a near relation of the Michaelmas-daisy that blooms in our gardens in September. Although we call this a daisy it is really an aster. The sea-asters I know on the Walberswick marshes are not much more than twelve inches high, but some specimens in some marshes reach a height of three feet. They are splendid flowers.

Perhaps the commonest of all the sea-shore flowers is the handsome YELLOW-HORNED POPPY. The thick, divided leaves are coarsely toothed and close to the stem. From June to October the bright yellow flowers of this gay poppy bloom steadily, but the petals soon fall and give place to long, narrow seed-pods, which sometimes grow to a length of twelve inches. The seeds in these extraordinary-looking pods contain much oil. Although this poppy is a cheerful sight in the shingle, I should not pick it because an unpleasant and nasty-smelling juice comes from the stalk when it is broken.

Lower down the beach, and perhaps actually within reach of the spray, grows a member of the parsley family called SEA-HOLLY. It is a pretty plant and blooms during the holiday season with a rounded head of bluish white flowers. The whole appearance of the plant is grey and, strangely enough, it will last a long time out of water.

There probably are other relations of the parsley–carrot group within walking distance, the best known of them being SAMPHIRE, which grows readily on both cliffs and sea-shore. Its smallish flowers are greenish white, with whorls of very narrow leaves round them. It has a strong smell, and in some places is still gathered for pickling.

Another relation of a well-known hedge flower is the SEA-CAMPION which has lovely white, star-shaped petals and usually grows in clumps even among the pebbles. Sometimes, however, it chooses a rocky crevice on the cliffs. You can see at once that it is a cousin of the bladder-campion.

SEA-SPURGE likes the sand-hills and blossoms from July to October. It has a rosette of small, yellowish green flowers rising above shiny, purple leaves. There are two curious things about this little flower which are worth remembering—the first is that when the stalks are broken, a milky juice which is said to be a good cure for warts comes out, and the other is that the leaves are the food of the very strange-looking caterpillar of the spurge hawk-moth. This caterpillar is rather rare, and is black with white and red spots arranged in lines.

Sooner or later our road will reach the sea-shore. Perhaps across a marsh or over the sand dunes or steeply down between the cliffs? It has always seemed strange to me that some plants can grow and flourish from crevices in the rocks or in the actual cliffs. The reason is that such plants that are frequently soaked with salt spray or sea water have to store what fresh water they can find in fleshy stems and thick, shiny leaves. You'll soon learn to recognize this sort of plant by its characteristics, and a typical one is samphire mentioned above.

On our journey down this road I've told you mostly about a few of the wild flowers you may find, but of course you will soon recognize some sea-birds and their mournful cries. You should also look out for some of the butterflies and moths that enjoy the sea air. I told you just now about the caterpillar of the SPURGE HAWK-MOTH, but you would be lucky to see the actual moth, because it is very rare and flies very quickly. Its small wings have a most beautiful rose tint.

Then there is a very tiny moth which is much more common, called the THRIFT CLEARWING, which hovers rather like a fly over the clumps of pink thrift.

But of course you may meet many common butterflies on the road to the sea just as frequently as you would see them miles inland. For instance, if our road goes over any chalk downs or along the chalk cliffs, you may see the CHALKHILL BLUE, sometimes in July but more likely in August, particularly in southern England. As its name suggests, this attractive little butterfly is silvery blue, usually with a dark border on the outer edges of the forewings.

Much more spectacular and unmistakable is the handsome PEACOCK which is usually on the wing in August and September. On each of its velvety, brownish red wings is the bold badge of a 'peacock's eye'. If you have seen a peacock with its tail spread wide, you will know what I mean by this. If you have not been so lucky, look at our splendid coloured picture. Peacock butterflies are fairly common and are often seen over cottage gardens and waste ground because the female lays her eggs under the young leaves of stinging nettles.

There is not really room to describe any more butterflies now, but if your road runs between hedgerows or is bordered with fields, you should look for the SMALL COPPER, the MEADOW BROWN and the ORANGE TIP, and many more besides.

Did you know that many of the butterflies which we see inland in our gardens and fluttering over the hedges may sometimes be seen crossing the sea, and that they come to us from great distances, as do the swallows and other migrant birds? You may easily see RED ADMIRALS or CLOUDED YELLOWS coming to us over the waves and up the road to the sea.

Every book must have an end and so must every holiday. When you have to say good-bye to the seaside for a while, remember that the tide, as it slips down the beach, will return. The restless sea will be waiting for you—beating against the rocks and cliffs, filling the pools again, hissing out over the shingle, smoothing the sand, bringing you treasures and reviving your memories.

Index

Acorn-barnacles, 12
Anemones, 11–13
Anglesey, 72
Angling, *see* Sea-angling
Arctic tern, 46
Atlantis, 3
Auks, 46

Bait, 31
Bardsey Island lighthouse, 57
Barnacles, 12; *see also* under kind
    of barnacle
Bathyscaphe, 2
Beach-flea, *see* Sand-hopper
Beachy Head lighthouse, 55
Beadlet, 12
Bell Rock lighthouse, 58
Berry Head lighthouse, 55
Birds, *see* Sea-birds
    migration of, 40
Bishop Rock lighthouse, 54
Black-headed gull, 42
Bladder-wrack seaweed, 16
Breeches-buoy, 63
Brill, 35, 37
Brittle starfish, 9
Butterflies, 82–3; *see also* under
    kind of butterfly

Cardium, 24
Chalkhill blue butterfly, 82
Chicken Rock lighthouse, 57
Cinque Ports, 67, 68
Clouded yellow butterflies, 83
Coast-Guards, H.M., 53, 60–4
Coast Life-Saving Corps, 61–4
Cockles, 24, 32
Cod, 29
Common gull, 44
Common sole, 36
Common tern, 45

Convolvulus, 80
Cork lightship, 60
Cormorants, 49
Cornish coast, 70–1
Cotton-spinner, 11
Crabs, 11, 29, 30, 32; *see also*
    under kind of crab
Crustacea, 11–14, 29
Cushion starfish, 10

Dabs, 29, 35, 36
Demersal fish, 29
Devon coast, 69–70, 71
Dogger Bank, 2
Dog-whelk, 25
Drifting, 30
Dungeness, 55, 68; lighthouse,
    54–6
Dunwich, 75, 81

Eddystone lighthouse, 55

Fingal's Cave, 73
Fish, 27–38
Fishing, *see* Sea-angling, drifting,
    trawling, seining
Flounders, 29, 35, 36
Flowers and plants, vii, 78–82
Fuchsia, 79
Fulmar, 51

Galloper lightship, 60
Gannet, 48
Geese: wild geese coming south,
    40
Goodwin, North, East and *South*,
    lightships, 60
Goodwin Sands, 60
Goose-barnacle, 12
Grace Darling, 57
Great black-backed gull, 42

Guillemot, 47
Gulf Stream, 4
Gulls, 34, 40–5; *see also* under
    kind of gull

Haddock, 29
Haisborough lightship, 60
Halibut, 37
Hartland Point lighthouse, 56
Hawthorn, 78
Hermit-crabs, 11
Herring, 29, 33
Herring-gull, 41
Holyhead Breakwater lighthouse
    57

Jelly-fish, 15

Kentish Knock lightship, 60
Kittiwake, 44

Lemina, 3
Lemon sole, 36
Lesser black-backed gull, 43
Life-boats, 53
Life-saving apparatus, 62–3
Lighthouses, 53–7
Lightships, 53, 57–60
Limpets, 23, 32
Little tern, 46
Lizard lighthouse, 54
Lobster, 14, 29, 30
Long-Sand lightship, 60
Longships lighthouse, 56
Longstone lighthouse, 57
Lugworm, 32
Lundy, 56

Mackerel, 29, 34
Manx shearwater, 50
Marram grass, 79–80
Masked crab, 11
May tree, 78
Meadow brown butterflies, 83
Menai Straits bridge, 72
Mollusca, 20–5, 29
Moon, pull of, on tides, 5
Mother Carey's Chickens, *see*
    Stormy petrel
Moths, 82

Mussels, 22, 29

Needles, The, lighthouse, 55, 69
Norfolk coast, 74–5

Orange-tip butterflies, 83
Orford Ness, 75
Oysters, 23, 29

Peacock butterflies, 83
Pelagic fish, 29
Periwinkle, 24
Petrels, 49–50
Piddock, 21
Pilchards, 29, 33
Pine, 78
Plaice, 29, 30, 35, 36
Pollack, 37
Prawns, 13–14, 29, 32
Puffins, 47, 51

Ragworm, 32
Razor-bill, 47
Razor-shell, 21, 32
Red admirals, 83
Rock sea-lavender, 80
Romney, Hythe and Dymchurch
    Light Railway, 56, 67
Romney Marsh, 67
Round Island lighthouse, 56

St. Catherine's lighthouse, 55, 69
Samphire, 81
Sand-hopper, 9
Sand-sedge, 79
Sand-stars, 10
Sandwich tern, 46
Sargasso Sea, 3–4
Sargassum, 3–4
Scallops, 23, 29
Scots pine, 78
Scottish coast, 72–3
Sea-anemones, *see* Anemones
Sea-angling, 31
Sea-asters, 81
Sea-bindweed, *see* Convolvulus
Sea-birds, 39–51; *see also* under
    kind of bird
Sea-buckthorn, 79
Sea-campion, 82

Sea-cucumbers, 10
Sea-holly, 81
Sea-lavender, 80
Seamew, *see* Common gull
Sea-pink, *see* Thrift
Sea-sedge, *see* Sand-sedge
Sea-spurge, 82
Seaweed, vii, 15–18; iodine from, 16
Sea-urchin, 10
Seining, 30
Seven Stones lightship, 60
Shag, 49
Shearwater, 50
Shells, vii, 19–26
Shore-crab, 11
Shrimps, 13, 29, 32
Skate, 37
Small copper butterflies, 83
Smalls lighthouse, 56
Snake-armed starfish, *see* Brittle starfish
Sole, 29, 30, 35, 36
South Foreland lighthouse, 56
South Stack lighthouse, 57
Sprats, 29
Spurge hawk-moth, 82
Stalked barnacle, *see* Goose-barnacle
Starfish, 9; *see also* under kind of starfish

Start Point lighthouse, 55
Stormy petrel, 49
Suffolk coast, 75
Sun starfish, 10

Tamarisk, 78
Tern, 34, 40, 45–6; *see also* under kind of tern
Thrift, 80
Thrift clearwing, 82
Tides, vii, 1, 2; 'gravitation' and tides, 5
Trawling, 29, 30–1
Trinity House, 53
Turbot, 29, 35, 36

Venus shells, 24
Viper-fish, *see* Weever

Weever, 15
Welsh coast, 71–2
Western Isles, 73
Whelks, 25
Whitby, 74
Whitebait, 29
Whiting, 29, 37
Wind, 6; from south-west, 78
Wolf Rock lighthouse, 54

Yellow-horned poppy, 81
Yorkshire coast, 73–4

Acknowledgments

The decorations in the text were drawn by M. P. McGuinness. The publishers are most grateful to the following for permission to reproduce the illustrations used in this book:

Associated Press for the black-and-white photographs of the trawler and trawling off Iceland; Harold Bastin for the black-and-white photographs of the sand-hoppers, sun star, sea-cucumber, brittle starfish, sea-spurge, sea-holly, yellow-horned poppy, sea-bindweed, sea-buckthorn, samphire, tamarisk, piddock, common periwinkles, common whelk, hawthorn, masked crab, great scallop, hermit-crab, lobster, acorn-barnacles, bladder-wrack, oyster and lugworm; A. Vincent Bibbings for the black-and-white photographs of the Berry Head lighthouse and Start Point lighthouse; Blackpool *Gazette and Herald* Ltd. for the black-and-white photograph of launching the Fleetwood lifeboat; British Oxygen Gases for the black-and-white photograph of the Sevenstones lightship; Central Office of Information for the two black-and-white photographs of coast-guard stations; Fox Photos for the black-and-white photograph of the Eddystone lighthouse; Keystone Press Agency for the black-and-white photographs of the herring boat and pilchard boat; W. Townsley Mitchell for the colour transparencies of the fuchsia, thrift, sea-lavender, sea-aster and sea-campion; L. Hugh Newman's Natural History Agency for the colour transparencies of the sea-anemones, common tern, peacock butterfly, cormorant, spurge hawk-moth, gannet, lesser black-backed gull, shags, herring-gull, jelly-fish, little tern, black-headed gull, kittiwakes, goose-barnacles, sea-urchin, arctic tern, red admiral, fulmar, puffins and the black-and-white photographs of the starfish, razor-shells, cockles and mussels by Walter J. C. Murray, the colour transparency of the thrift clearwing by S. Dalton, and the black-and-white photographs of the shore-crab, shrimp and prawn by Ray Palmer; R. Perry for the black-and-white photograph of the common gull by C. A. Gibson Hill; Alan Richardson for the black-and-white photographs of the great black-backed gull, the razor-bill and the guillemot.

The frontispiece photograph is of Tintagel, Cornwall, and is reproduced by permission of Central Press Photos.